CW01460804

MEMORIES OF CHOIRS AND CLOISTERS

Brewer, photographed on 18 January 1926 by the leading society photographic firm of Bassano. Lady Brewer was photographed the same day.

© National Portrait Gallery, London.
Reproduced by permission.

MEMORIES OF CHOIRS AND CLOISTERS

FIFTY YEARS OF MUSIC

A. Herbert Brewer

Edited by John Morehen

First published in 1931 by
John Lane The Bodley Head Ltd
London

This edition first published in 2015 by
Stainer & Bell Ltd
PO Box 110, Victoria House
23 Gruneisen Road
London N3 1DZ
www.stainer.co.uk

© Copyright 2015 John Morehen

All rights reserved. This book is copyright under the Berne Convention.
It is fully protected by the British Copyright, Designs and Patents Act 1988
and any subsequent amending legislation. No part of the work may be
reproduced, stored in a retrieval system, or transmitted in any form
by any means, electronic, mechanical, photocopying or otherwise,
without the prior permission of Stainer & Bell Ltd.

Every effort has been made to trace all owners of copyright;
if any have unwittingly remained undiscovered, the
publishers offer apologies and will gladly make
full acknowledgment in any future edition.

British Library Cataloguing-in-Publication Data
A catalogue record of this book is available from the British Library

Catalogue No. B946

ISBN 978 0 85249 946 7

Printed in Great Britain by Caligraving Ltd

CONTENTS

LIST OF ILLUSTRATIONS

ORIGINAL FOREWORD

My husband, who was often asked by his friends to write his reminiscences, amused himself by jotting down, from time to time, these recollections and anecdotes. He never revised them or recast them, so they must not be taken to represent his final intentions, but it has been thought that they may interest or entertain those who knew him, and they are now published with no further alteration than a few explanatory notes and verbal corrections, and with an Epilogue which includes some personal recollections by W. H. Reed, M.V.O.

Ethel M. Brewer

REVISER'S NOTE

The 1931 edition of Brewer's *Memories* lacks chapter headings; those provided here are my own, and are intended to convey only the broad subject area(s) of the individual chapters. Because of the format of the original edition Brewer's paragraphs were shorter, and therefore more numerous. I have taken advantage of the new format to merge many of Brewer's paragraphs in order to avoid excessive disjointedness. I have also modernized the spellings, word forms, punctuation, composers' names, *etc.* in accordance with current conventions. Similarly, I have rationalized some of Brewer's more eccentric punctuation (or lack of it). Original quotations, however, have generally been allowed to stand, even if this results in occasional inconsistencies with the main text.

Of the eight illustrations in the original edition, only the photograph of Brewer at the console of the restored Gloucester Cathedral organ (1920) has been retained. The opportunity has been taken to include three additional photographs which were not included in the 1931 edition.

I would like to acknowledge my indebtedness to many friends and correspondents who have made helpful suggestions or who have supplied information, in particular Stephen Banfield, Hilary Davan Wetton, Paul Hale, Peter Horton, Donald Hunt, Nicolas Kynaston, Jonathan MacKechnie-Jarvis, Beverley Matthews, Paul Rodmell, Lucy Royal-Dawson, Richard Shephard and John Whittle. To Elizabeth Jack I owe special thanks for providing me with details from many relevant documents in the Gloucestershire Archives. Nobody who writes on any aspect of the Three Choirs Festival can fail to owe a large debt of gratitude to Anthony Boden, whose definitive history – *Three Choirs: A History of the Festival* (1992) – will undoubtedly prove to be of particular interest in this the Festival's 300th anniversary year.

NEWARK-ON-TRENT   *John Morehen*
2015

viii

MEMORIES OF CHOIRS AND CLOISTERS

– 1 –

Early upbringing in Gloucester

At a very early age I was passionately fond of music, a taste which was fostered by my parents, especially my mother. My father,[1] being no mean performer on more than one wind instrument, led me to take an interest in orchestral music and military bands when I was quite small. One of my earliest recollections (I had hardly got beyond the toddling stage) is of following the Gloucester Artillery Band on a march out to Rudford, a village some three miles from Gloucester. When I was discovered I was taken to the house where the band was being entertained, and helped to devour the good things which had been prepared for them. How I got back to Gloucester I cannot remember, but I have a dim recollection of being carried on the big drum.

My first pianoforte master was John Hooper, a man whose musical taste was far in advance of his time, and he was also a violinist of some ability. He held the post of organist at the Roman Catholic church in Gloucester,[2] and I often accompanied him and sat beside him on the organ stool and watched him play. A habit of his which impressed itself on my young mind was his passion for taking snuff. Some fifty years later when Elgar was staying with me and was in a reminiscent mood, he referred to Hooper, whom he had met in his younger days, as a man who possessed undoubted ability.[3]

It was my ambition to become a chorister, and I took the first opportunity of joining a church choir. The church (St Mark's) was not noted in any way for its music; the organist was an amateur, a very poor performer, and more accustomed to act as pianist

---

1   According to Watkins Shaw, *The Succession of Organists of the Chapel Royal and the Cathedrals of England and Wales from c.1538* (Oxford, 1991), p.128, Brewer's father – also Alfred – was a Gloucester hotel proprietor. However, the Scholars' Register at the Royal College of Music describes him as Clerk at Gloucester Probate Court.
2   St Peter's Church, London Road, Gloucester, was consecrated in 1868.
3   Contemporary trade directories list a John Hooper, 'professor of music', as living at 1 Oxford Street, Gloucester, which is within walking distance of St Peter's Church.

at dances than to play church services. The organ, with worn-out mechanism and no variety of tone, was in a deplorable state.[4] Arriving at the church rather early one Sunday morning I found a large black cat wandering about the churchyard. I enticed him into the vestry, not with the intention of clothing him with a surplice, but of adding variety to the tone of the organ. With this object in view I placed 'Master Pussy' in one of the big, open pedal pipes. No unusual sound disturbed the voluntary because the organist had not used this particular stop, but at the beginning of the *Venite* most unearthly noises proceeded from the organ. The more stops that were added the more weird became the sounds. At last the organist, thoroughly bewildered, stopped playing and the choir ceased singing. By this time Pussy had climbed to the top of the open diapason pedal pipe, and, thoroughly scared, took a flying leap into the centre of the church; then, successfully evading all efforts on the part of the congregation to capture him, flew out of the building. The schoolchildren were immensely delighted with this unusual addition to the service, but the vicar and churchwardens viewed the matter in a different light, and the result was my suspension from the choir for a fortnight. As I did not return to the church at the end of that time the authorities waited on me and asked me to return, but my youthful *amour-propre* had suffered, and they saw me no more at that place of worship.[5]

Some time later my brother[6] and I competed for vacancies in the Cathedral choir. The then Organist, C. H. Lloyd,[7] was not impressed with my singing, but he decided to admit us both into the choir because, as he said, my performance on the piano displayed musicianship, and I could also look after my young brother, who, in his opinion, was likely to become an excellent singer. Such an

---

4   By coincidence the present editor also was a chorister at St Mark's, Kingsholm. Under Harry Dawes, Director of Music at The Crypt Grammar School from 1931 to 1967, the choir became renowned regionally, and regularly deputized for the Cathedral choir. The church's three-manual Hill organ, built in 1907, was fully restored by J. W. Walker in 1954.

5   Brewer's claim that "... they saw me no more at that place of worship" is not quite true, for he returned there at least once – for his wedding to Ethel Mary Bruton in September 1894!

6   Charles Sidney Brewer (1868–1943).

7   Charles Harford Lloyd (1849–1919) was organist of Gloucester Cathedral from 1876 to 1882. He features prominently in Brewer's *Memories*.

instance proves how difficult it is to forecast the future of boys' voices. My brother's voice never developed to any extent, but within a year I was head chorister and solo boy, and chosen to sing in a Quartet at a Festival with Madame Patey,[8] Edward Lloyd[9] and Charles Santley.[10]

When C. H. Lloyd became organist in 1876, the standard of singing in the Cathedral choir was at a very low ebb. Wesley[11] was essentially an organist and composer, and not a choir trainer or conductor. In fact, towards the end of his time the training of the choristers was left in the hands of one of the lay-clerks. When a full rehearsal of the choir took place the men made no attempt to sing out but just whispered their parts. This tradition continued for some time after Wesley's death, and when a new lay-clerk was appointed, who showed his zeal and enthusiasm by really singing his part at a rehearsal as it should be sung, his colleagues remonstrated with him at the close of the practice for using his voice unnecessarily!

The choristers were educated at the College School (now known as the King's School), but they had not the advantages that the present boys enjoy. The education was of the scantiest on account of the time spent in the Cathedral at practices and morning and afternoon services, all of which came out of school hours. In spite of this the choristers competed and more than held their own with the ordinary schoolboy. They not only passed the Oxford and Cambridge local examinations, but won open scholarships at the Universities direct from the school. Some achieved still further renown, a notable instance being the present distinguished headmaster of Westminster School, Dr Costley-White.[12] The school buildings were

---

8 The contralto Janet Monach Patey (1842–94) was known as 'the English Alboni'.
9 Edward Lloyd (1845–1927). Together with Sims Reeves (see p.139, fn.1) Lloyd was one of the leading tenors of his day. One of Lloyd's last appearances was in the first performance of Elgar's *The Dream of Gerontius* in Birmingham Town Hall (1900).
10 (Sir) Charles Santley (1834–1922), the distinguished baritone, achieved international fame, especially in opera. He appeared in the first English performance of Gounod's *Faust* in 1863.
11 Samuel Sebastian Wesley (1810–76), successively organist of Hereford and Exeter cathedrals, Leeds Parish Church and Winchester Cathedral before being appointed to Gloucester Cathedral in 1865.
12 Harold Costley-White (1878–1966) was Head Master of Westminster School from 1919 to 1937. Although Brewer did not live to see it, Costley-White returned to Gloucester as Dean from 1938 to 1953.

very inadequate. Nearly all the forms were held in one room, and the pandemonium caused by the masters competing with each other in their attempts to drive the rudiments of Latin, Greek and arithmetic into the heads of the boys, all at the same time, was indescribable. But it had one advantage – it forced on the boys the habit of concentration. My experience has been that boys who have a knowledge of music and a keen ear generally have a great advantage in learning over boys who have no sense of sound or pitch. I have found this to be the experience of such headmasters as Dr Wood of Harrow,[13] Dr Lyttelton[14] of Eton and also Dr Costley-White.

There was one master in the school who took more interest in my music than in my ordinary studies. He promised me ten shillings[15] as soon as I could play a Bach fugue on the organ. In those days my pocket-money was very limited so I lost no time in learning it, but I regret to say I never received the ten shillings. There are always Cathedral devotees who wish to lavish kindness on the choristers. I recall one who elected to gratify this inclination during service. She – needless to say it was a lady – occupied a pew next to the choir. Her close proximity to the boys proved too great a temptation for her and she tossed an orange to the nearest boy. Her aim, unfortunately, was not very sure, [and] the orange missed its mark and went rolling down the centre of the choir.

There was a pew, in those far-off days, set apart for the Canon who was in residence, and in this his wife and family sat. On the opposite side there was one which was known as the out-of-residence pew for the relatives of the Canons who were not in residence. I well remember on a Monday morning – it was the first of April – the wife of a Canon, who had been in residence during the first three months of the year, suddenly realized during the singing of the psalms that her husband had gone out of residence on the previous day. She immediately picked up her belongings – umbrella, cloak, books, etc. – and solemnly walked across to the out-of-residence pew. What

---

13   The Rev'd Dr Joseph Wood (1842–1921), Headmaster of Tonbridge (1890–98) and of Harrow School (1899–1910), and subsequently Canon Residentiary of Rochester Cathedral.
14   The Rev'd The Hon. Edward Lyttelton (1855–1942), Headmaster of Eton from 1905 to 1916.
15   i.e. 50p in decimal currency.

made it all the more ludicrous was the fact that she was the only member of the congregation.

There were two Minor Canons who used to afford the boys a good deal of amusement. One was not very clear in his articulation, having great difficulty with certain words. When intoning the service he always said, "O Lord, *shave* the Queen," and "O Lord, *shave* Thy people." But imagine our surprise at hearing the other Minor Canon, a keen sportsman, when reading the Lesson, say, "Now Barabbas was a rabbit!"[16]

One of the Canons had great antipathy to any music by Mendelssohn. In those days the weekly list was written out and not printed as it is now, and when *If with all your hearts*[17] was down to be sung, Handel's name was always substituted for Mendelssohn's on this particular Canon's scheme. Towards the end of his life this same Canon became so infirm and short-sighted that he read the Lessons from his stall. It was his custom to follow each line with his finger, and on one occasion, being more short-sighted than usual, he said, "And David said unto Jonathan" – long pause – "I've lost my place!" Another Canon used to find fault with the choir whenever *Grant us Thy Peace*[18] by Mendelssohn was sung because, as he complained, they did not end it together. It will be remembered that it ends in imitation, the tenors and basses singing two bars later exactly the same phrase as the trebles and altos.

On one occasion, when entertaining the senior members of the choir to supper, the Dean (Mr Law)[19] laid special stress on the excellence of the celery served up from the Deanery garden. Proud of its quality, he asked his guests what they thought of his 'celery' (which sounded to the lay-clerks' ears like 'salary'), and added, "I raise it myself." Whereupon a lay-clerk, taking courage in both hands, remarked, "I wish, Mr Dean, you would raise mine!"

It was with the greatest sorrow and regret, when my voice broke, that I left my musical nursery. I had been head boy as well as solo boy for about four years, and fully appreciated the position. There

16 "Now Barabbas was a robber." (*John* 18, v.40).
17 From *Elijah*.
18 *Verleih uns Frieden gnädiglich* (1831).
19 Henry Law (1797–1884), Dean from 1862 until his death. His father, George Henry Law (1761–1845) was Bishop successively of Chester and of Bath and Wells.

can be no better training for a young musician than the life of a cathedral chorister, especially in one of the cathedrals of the Three Choirs. Here they are not confined to Gibbons in F and Tallis in D minor,[20] but are able to keep abreast of the times and learn the works of the most modern composers. The Festivals make this valuable experience possible.

In my opinion the ability to read music at sight is not on such a high level now as it was fifty years ago. I cannot help thinking that one of the reasons is the general use of the vocal score instead of the single voice part. In those days most of the music consisted of single voice parts in manuscript. A few cathedrals possessed copies of either Barnard or Boyce, but, generally speaking, vocal scores were exceedingly rare.[21] There is not the slightest doubt that the best readers of music in this or any other country are orchestral players. They have no score to help them, and therefore cannot see what is happening in the other parts, but have to rely entirely on themselves and their single part.

---

20 i.e. Gibbons's 'Short' (First) Service and Tallis's 'Dorian' (or 'Short') Service respectively.

21 Brewer is a little confused here, as Barnard's collection (*The First Book of Selected Church Musick*, 1641) is not in score but in ten separate partbooks. It is very unlikely, in any case, that any choirs would still have been performing from Barnard partbooks as late as the nineteenth century.

- 2 -

First professional appointments (c.1878-82)

My first experience as an organist happened to be in Gloucester prison; not by way of punishment, but to help the Governor, Major Knox,[1] out of a difficulty. I well remember my terror when once inside the gates. The head-warder gave me a key which was to admit me through all the doors leading to the chapel. I had an idea that perhaps on my way there I might be attacked by prisoners, so I carefully left each door unlocked as I passed through, in case I wished to beat a hasty retreat. Unfortunately for me the Governor followed close on my heels, and when he discovered what had happened he sent for me and used language which will not bear repetition.

The chaplain at the prison was a tall, flabby-looking old man with an unkempt beard, whose general unhealthy appearance gave one the impression of a diet of hot-buttered toast. It was this gentleman's duty to look after the souls of those confined within the gaol. At that time the idea of reducing the prison to a lower grade was in contemplation. This meant, in so far as he was concerned, a considerable reduction in salary, as the chaplain would not be engaged as a 'whole timer', but would be expected to do outside work in addition, and to this he strongly objected. He aired his grievances to the Governor, who replied that he quite understood the wish of the authorities: crime was decreasing, and there were very few prisoners. "Ah," said the chaplain, "there is as much crime now as ever there was. But the fact is the police can't catch them; it is they who are at fault." A few days later the chaplain again saw the Governor, who was in a very despondent mood. Being asked the reason of his despondency, he deplored the fact that the prison was full up. "Come, come," said the chaplain, rubbing his hands and brightening visibly, "this is much better!"

---

1   James Knox, Governor of Gloucester Prison for almost twenty years, later served as Governor of Armley and Wandsworth prisons.

About the same time I was asked to undertake Sunday work as organist at Painswick, a small town on the Cotswold Hills about six miles from Gloucester. These week-ends I looked forward to with pleasure. Mr McCrea,[2] the vicar, was a wealthy bachelor, who did himself well, and I, on these occasions, shared the good things with him. The organ was a poor one and the choir even worse. During my first service I heard sounds like the pattering of hail-stones. This greatly puzzled me as it happened to be a bright summer's day; but I soon discovered that some of the choir-boys on the side opposite the organ were using pea-shooters. Whether they were trying to shoot me or the organ pipes I never found out. Their length of service as choristers did not go beyond that Sunday.

When still a chorister I occasionally deputized for the organist of Highnam Church. It was then that I first met Hubert Parry. His father, Gambier Parry, was still alive, and occupied Highnam Court.[3] He was not only an able painter – the result of his genius is to be seen in Ely Cathedral as well as at Gloucester – but he was devoted to music and did much to advance the art in Gloucestershire. He took a very prominent part in the management of the Three Choirs Festivals, and was also President of the Gloucester Choral Society. His generosity was boundless. He built and endowed a hospital for children and also the beautiful church on the Highnam estate. The church is after the style of Salisbury Cathedral, and the mosaics and frescoes attract many visitors to the spot. On the death of his father Sir Hubert came into the property and, whenever he was at home on a Sunday, would don a surplice and take his place in the choir.

My first organistship dates back to April, 1881, when I was appointed to St Catharine's Church.[4] It was the most fashionable church in Gloucester at the time, and it was no uncommon sight to see a long queue outside the church on Sundays before the doors

---

2   The Rev'd Herbert Henry McCrea (1847–1902).

3   Highnam Court is located about two miles from Gloucester to the North West. Thomas Gambier Parry (1816–88) strongly discouraged his children from pursuing music as a profession. See Boden, *Three Choirs: A History of the Festival* (Stroud, 1992), pp.98 & 102.

4   St Catharine's Church, London Road, Gloucester, was consecrated in 1868. Its organ – a single-manual instrument by Henry Bryceson, with pedals – is described in Roy Williamson, *The Organs of Gloucester, Tewkesbury and Cirencester, from the XVth Century* (Cheltenham, 1991), p.49.

were opened. The vicar, Canon Mayne,[5] was a popular man, but the chief attraction was the choir, which was easily the best church choir in the city. My predecessor had had the sense not to ape the cathedral service, which was to be heard within a stone's throw of St Catharine's, but aimed at a good parochial service, in which the congregation could take part. In fact, it was an ideal parish church service.

My appointment caused a commotion amongst the junior members of the choir; I was fifteen and a half at the time and probably younger than many of the choir-boys, and they strongly objected to the head cathedral chorister lording it over them. So they played a low-down trick on me at my first service. The organist's seat was in full view of the congregation, and feeling full of pride at finding myself in such a prominent position I remained there throughout the service. It was fortunate that I did, for after my concluding voluntary I found it difficult to tear myself away from the stool. The little demons had plastered the seat with cobbler's wax!

Following the example of most young composers my first effort in composition was a setting of the evening canticles, and it was for the choir of St Catharine's that I wrote it. With the venturesome of extreme youth I rushed into print and published it without consulting those who would have assuredly advised otherwise. The temptation of a sure performance and the delight of seeing one's work in print were too much for me, and I fell.[6] I remained at St Catharine's only until the following November, when I succeeded G. R. Sinclair[7] as organist of St Mary-de-Crypt.[8] More than one organist who eventually gained distinction in the world of music had

---

5   The Rev'd Jonathan Mayne (1838–1912) was appointed Curate of St Catharine's in 1867 and Vicar in 1869. He became an Honorary Canon of Gloucester Cathedral in 1884. His son, The Very Rev'd William Cyril Mayne (1877–1962), was Dean of Carlisle from 1943 to 1959.
6   This early setting of the evening canticles is something of an enigma. Brewer's earliest published setting of the evening canticles appears to be his setting in B flat, published by Novello, Ewer & Co. in 1894.
7   George Robertson Sinclair (1863–1917) was later organist of Truro Cathedral (1880–89) and of Hereford Cathedral (1889–1917). As 'G.R.S.' he was the inspiration for variation 11 of Elgar's *Variations on an Original Theme* (Op.36).
8   The historic church of St Mary-de-Crypt is located on Southgate Street, close to Gloucester city centre.

occupied this position: Dr James Taylor,[9] organist of New College, Oxford, and of the University, held this post; and Dr Kendrick Pyne[10] combined its duties with those of assistant to Dr Wesley.

George Robertson Sinclair was sixteen and I fourteen when we met as pupils under Lloyd in the organ-loft of Gloucester Cathedral. Our friendship grew as years went by, and we were drawn closer in our work when we found ourselves respectively Conductors of the Three Choirs Festivals at Hereford and Gloucester. As I look back I realize what a splendid training and preparation for these responsible positions we had as boys under the guiding hand of our old friend and master, C. H. Lloyd. I do not know how far it affected our friendship, but in those days we were so alike that we were often mistaken for each other, and the outward resemblance was a symbol of the deep friendship existing between us from our boyhood until Sinclair's death on February 7th, 1917.

A short time before Sinclair died an organist met me in London and, mistaking me for him, said, "I hear Brewer is in Town; I want to know where he can be found." Again, when we were examining together for the Royal College of Organists,[11] a similar case occurred. I had met with an accident and injured my leg, and a musician, who might have been expected to know us apart, in wishing Sinclair good-bye, expressed the hope that his leg would soon be better. Times out of number have I been congratulated on the performances at the Hereford Festivals when Sinclair had been conducting. Few enjoyed the joke more than he did. The interest and enthusiasm Sinclair displayed in connection with the Three Choirs Festivals were unbounded. His playing of an organ concerto at the Gloucester Festivals was an outstanding feature. He was a brilliant executant with few equals.

During our training at Gloucester there was an old blower who took the keenest interest in everything we did, and was not afraid to criticize our performances. 'Old Michael', as he was called,

---

9   James Taylor (1833–1900) was briefly organist of St Mary-de-Crypt in 1850. See Shaw, *The Succession of Organists*, p.393.
10   James Kendrick Pyne (1852–1938) was briefly organist of Chichester Cathedral (1873). After working in the USA for a short period he returned to England on his appointment as organist of Manchester Cathedral (1876–1908).
11   At that time the College occupied prestigious premises in Kensington Gore, opposite the Royal Albert Hall.

delighted in telling people how many organists he had turned out, and was especially proud of Sinclair and Brewer. When I was leaving Gloucester I noticed one day that he was very thoughtful and evidently had something on his mind. I asked him what troubled him. He expressed his regret at my leaving, and said how anxious he was to possess my photograph. When he heard that his request was to be granted, he exclaimed, evidently wishing that I should not be put to any expense, "You might take it out in blowing!"

The cathedral organ, as it was in those days, had been rebuilt by Henry Willis in 1862 during the organistship of John Amott.[12] Amott was not a very distinguished musician, and his ability as an organist was, so one of his old choristers told me, of an elementary character. The pedals were rarely used, and when he did play on them he would allow the choristers, as a special favour, to go to the organ-loft to see how it was done. As a rule a board was placed over the pedals on which his feet rested. It was possible to get all the pedal effects on the manuals, the Great organ manual being carried down to CCC, an arrangement I have never seen or heard of anywhere else. The result was that every stop on the Great organ – there were eleven – had its own pedal bass. The draw stops were of various sizes and lengths, the one pedal stop, labelled 'Pedal Pipes', coming out a considerable length and dropping with a catch to prevent it flying back.

The instrument was originally built by Harris[13] in 1665, but it is doubtful whether the work was really completed then, as early entries of repairs and alterations follow in the Chapter records. The bellows, for instance, had not been encased and the record goes on to say that a sum of half a crown was "paid Mr Jordan for medicynes for the ratts that troubled the organ bellace." This seems to have led to the casing in of the bellows, according to a further entry, in 1667. The case and decoration of the pipes stand unaltered since it was erected.[14]

---

12 Amott (1799–1865) was organist of Gloucester Cathedral from 1832 until his death.

13 Thomas Harris (d.c.1684) also built the organ at Worcester Cathedral at about the same time. Further work was carried out at Gloucester by Henry Willis in 1847 and 1889.

14 The organ has undergone considerable restoration since Brewer's death, most notably in 1971 by Hill, Norman and Beard, and in 1999 by Nicholson.

Whilst speaking of the organ I cannot refrain from relating an amusing experience which happened to a friend of mine when practising. The door being left open the loft was accessible to anyone who wished to ascend. A countryman with a young friend of the opposite sex, whilst wandering round the cathedral, noticed the door ajar, and walked up into the loft. They watched my friend play, and, after a time, the country yokel, evidently wishing to impress the young lady with his knowledge of music, said, "Three rows of keys, I see; treble, (h)alto and bass, I suppose!"

It was not my good fortune to know S. S. Wesley personally, but he was well known to me by sight. He was often to be seen pacing up and down the College Green in front of his house dangling a glove by a finger-end, evidently thinking out some musical problem. He came to Gloucester in 1865. His anthems will ever remain memorials of his great genius. He understood how to get to the heart of his text and illustrate its inner meaning. In many ways he was a disappointed and soured man. He received little, if any, sympathy or encouragement over his writings, and it was only through the influence of Dean Garnier of Winchester,[15] to whom the volume is dedicated, that the great monument of his wonderful talent – a book of twelve anthems – came into the possession of the art-loving world in 1853. It was evidently his intention to follow up this collection with others, as this book is marked Volume I, but nothing further, to my knowledge, appeared.

Wesley was a keen fisherman and there are many stories told of him in this connection. On one occasion, when he was unconsciously(?) poaching, he was discovered and taken before the owner, who, on realizing the captive's identity, exclaimed, "Oh, Dr Wesley, you are the very man I have been wishing to meet. I have just built an organ in my house and I want you to play on it." Wesley was apparently obliging, but, considering it a breach of etiquette, afterwards sent in a bill for ten guineas. The reply was a *contra* account for fifteen guineas for a day's fishing. A Canon's wife saw him one day carrying an enormous carriage umbrella rolled up, and drew his attention to its size. He replied, "Madam, I'm aware of it; you see it is going to have a lot of little parasols." Here is a

---

15   Thomas Garnier (1776–1873), Dean of Winchester from 1840 to 1872.

characteristic remark of his: "Why should we not have monuments to perpetuate the fame of those who *neglect* their duty as well as those who perform it?"

Soon after his appointment to Gloucester Wesley was asked to conduct a Ladies' Society which had been organized by Mrs Ellicott,[16] the wife of the Bishop, the rehearsals being held at the Palace. But his conductorship lasted only a few minutes, for, after hearing them sing two or three bars, he banged the lid of the piano down and rushed from the room shouting "Cats!" It is a fact that once, at a Festival performance, he was so carried away by the music that he put his baton down and went to sleep. He had a keen sense of humour, which, mercifully, is rarely lacking in musicians. On one occasion he told the choristers that he would give half a crown to the boy who could find 'A flat' on a tombstone in the Cloisters. They lost no time in making a thorough search of the Cloisters. One bright boy discovered it – G. Sharp, Sculptor, Gloucester.[17] The chorister who won the half-crown told me the story himself many years afterwards.

Whilst organist of Exeter Cathedral[18] Wesley fell into disgrace one day for playing *Rule, Britannia* on the organ when he had been asked to play the National Anthem. His excuse, when questioned about it, was that he had informed the blowers of the Dean's request, but they had persisted in blowing *Rule, Britannia* into the organ. History does not relate if this explanation satisfied the Dean and Chapter. His appointment to Gloucester came as a surprise to his many friends. On the death of Amott, the Dean and Chapter consulted Wesley with regard to a successor, and much to their astonishment he expressed the wish to be a candidate himself. Their surprise was as great, so one of the Canons told me, as if the Archbishop of Canterbury had applied for a Minor Canonry. On the recommendation of Mr Gladstone[19] Wesley was offered the honour of knighthood, with the alternative of a Civil List pension of £100

---

16 For Constantia Ellicott's involvement in the Three Choirs Festival see pp.63–5 below.
17 There may well be more than one such tombstone, for that of Jane and Emma Evans in the North Cloister is inscribed 'G. SHARP. GLOSTER'.
18 1835–41.
19 William Gladstone served four terms as Liberal Prime Minister between 1868 and 1894.

per annum, for his distinguished services to church music. He chose the latter, remarking that it was a nice little nest-egg. This pension was continued to his widow.

The following characteristic letter was sent by him to the Chapter Clerk soon after his appointment to Gloucester:

October 3rd

Dear Sir

I have been desirous to know if you would repair a window of our hall passage roof-light. It is broken by a fall of mortar from the roof. The rain has damaged my furniture – floorcloth etc. I mean; and whenever it rains we have to procure things to catch the water.

I have made several applications to you about it and still have to ask whether you will correct this defect or whether you think it is my business and not the Dean and Chapter's. If the latter, I could easily get it done and send you the bill. The roof of the house is bad and I have suffered much loss. Mr Foljames[20] advised (at first when repairing the house) a new roof.

I want to leave home and must get this matter settled previously.

I am yours truly
S. S. Wesley

Another letter written to Mrs Ellicott relating to the organ is of special interest:

Sept: 29th 1875

Dear Mrs. Ellicott

I feel it to be most kind of you to have given your attention to the Cathedral Organ, and to have shown a willingness to improve things, but, deplorable as things

---

20 Thomas Fulljames (1808–74) was Diocesan Surveyor. See B. G. Carne, 'Thomas Fulljames, 1808–74, Surveyor, Architect and Civil Engineer', *Transactions of the Bristol and Gloucestershire Archaeological Society*, 113 (1995), pp.7–20. Fulljames designed the casework of the organ built by John Nicholson for the Shire Hall, Gloucester, in 1849/50.

are, I feel I ought to offer an opinion to the effect of not spending money in making any portion of the present mechanism better.

Anything good and new would not suit the old portion which would not be retained, or used, if the Instrument were put right thoroughly, and in doing that, only the best of the pipes would be valuable to the Dean and Chapter. The organ-builder should allow something for parts he could use up for smaller organs. I think that the right course is for the friends of Church Music to receive a circular containing a preliminary list of subscribers to the Organ Fund.

My small beginning – 10 guineas – may be introduced! We soon got more than was wanted at Winchester, and I doubt not we should do so here. Mr Ellicott's trying the organ will enable him to judge of its shortcomings.

Ever yours faithfully
S. S. Wesley

Wesley's hopes were not realized, for his advice to the Dean and Chapter was ignored and no appeal was made. The organ remained in the same condition until 1888.

He died in the Organist's house in Millers[21] Green on April 19th, 1876, and is buried in the old cemetery at Exeter. There is a tablet to his memory in the north aisle of the nave of Exeter Cathedral and a stained glass window in the South Chantry (the musicians' corner) of the Lady Chapel of Gloucester Cathedral, where a similar memorial has recently been placed to his successor, C. H. Lloyd.[22]

A familiar character in musical circles in Gloucester was John Hunt.[23] He was a tenor lay-clerk in the Cathedral choir and helped Dr Wesley in training the choristers. He was a very refined gentleman of amiable disposition and portly build.

A regular performer at the Choral Society's concerts was an elderly Peer, who attended the concerts clad in a long coat reaching

---

21 Brewer's preferred spelling 'Millers', without an apostrophe, has been retained here, although for his vocal suite *Miller's Green* he adopted the singular possessive form.
22 In 1930 Brewer himself was so honoured. See p.180 below.
23 John Hunt (1832–90), Sub-Sacrist at Gloucester Cathedral, lived at 2 Palace Yard.

to his ankles, which resembled a dressing-gown more than anything else. His enthusiasm, alas, exceeded his ability as a violinist. During a performance a professional, who happened to be sharing the same desk, said: "Excuse me, my lord, I think your violin is a little bit out of tune." The old gentleman took no notice but went on playing. The professional drew his attention to the fact; whereupon he took his violin down and felt the strings and, turning to his companion, said "I never have them any tighter!"

Another Gloucester worthy was J. W. Rippon,[24] a professional viola player who, in my youthful days, took his place at a viola desk at the Three Choirs Festival. In an interview after his last festival he spoke of his viola as an extraordinary instrument: it rarely required tuning. He declared that at the Festival which had just concluded he had tuned his viola at the beginning of the week and had had no occasion to touch the pegs during the whole of the Festival!

It almost equals an experience of my own when a young lady violinist applied for an engagement at my first Festival. Before making a decision I asked her to come and play to me, and, greatly to my surprise, I found that she had not advanced beyond the first position. The audacity of the candidate aroused my curiosity, and, wishing to soften my refusal, I inquired the make of her violin. To my amazement she replied: "It is a Stradivarius; it was specially made for me." This left me speechless, and I turned away to hide my amusement. Meanwhile she was packing up her rare instrument, and, noticing her ineffectual attempts to close the case, I offered my assistance. "Oh," she said, "I think it will shut more easily if I take my shoes out." She had placed a pair of shoes inside the case on the top of her unique Stradivarius!

About the time I left the choir it was decided that I should enter for the local examination of the Royal Academy of Music. The examiner was a composer of much sugary drawing-room music suggestive of antimacassars and schoolgirl ringlets. It did not take me long to discover that his knowledge of the organ was strictly limited. Almost the first thing he did was to ask me to play a chord on the pedals! I cautiously pulled out all the mixtures, fifteenths, twelfths and other piercing stops and managed to play two notes with each foot. The old gentleman, who had been sitting beside me,

---

24   John Wyles Rippon (1824–1901), of Midland Road, Gloucester.

was so frightened by the hideous noise that he fell off the seat, and passed me with honours.

– 3 –

Oxford (1882–5)

It was during the summer of 1882 that Lloyd was offered the position of organist at Christ Church, Oxford, on the resignation of Dr Corfe.[1] The then Dean, Dr Liddell,[2] had sought the advice of Dr Stainer,[3] who strongly recommended Lloyd for the appointment. The latter hesitated a good deal about relinquishing the Gloucester post on account of the prominence given it by the Three Choirs Festivals. As there was some doubt about Lloyd's acceptance, Stainer advised, in the event of Lloyd declining it, that the post should be offered to T. B. Strong,[4] a young Christ Church man, who had just taken his Arts degree.

Pressure was brought to bear and, eventually, Lloyd accepted it. Stainer's reason for urging Lloyd to return to Oxford was that he thought it inadvisable for a young man – he was then thirty-two – to settle down in a provincial town where there was no competition. But Stainer must have overlooked the value of the Festivals and of the outlet they gave to a man so full of energy and enthusiasm as Lloyd was; to say nothing of the opportunities they provided for a man with a gift for composition, and Lloyd's gift as a composer was certainly above the average.

Had Lloyd refused Christ Church and Strong accepted it, the musical profession would have been the richer and the Church the poorer in consequence. Strong had gained a scholarship from Westminster and had had a brilliant career at Oxford. He was a first-rate pianist and an excellent executant on the organ, but fate had

---

1 Charles William Corfe (1814–83) was organist of Christ Church Cathedral from 1846 to 1882.
2 Henry George Liddell (1811–98), classical scholar and Dean of Christ Church from 1855 to 1891. His daughter Alice was the subject of Lewis Carroll's *Alice in Wonderland* and other writings.
3 Sir John Stainer (1840–1901), organist of St Paul's Cathedral from 1872 to 1888.
4 Dr Thomas Banks Strong (1861–1944) later became Bishop of Oxford (see below, p.162). He was an early patron of Sir William Walton.

decreed that music was not to be his calling. Eventually he became Dean of the Cathedral, at which his great gifts as a musician qualified him to be organist. Surely a unique record!

Strong did much for music in the University and his influence had a lasting effect. He was a great supporter of the University Musical Club – a Club which was founded by Lloyd in his undergraduate days. Parry, who was at Oxford at the same time, also gave Lloyd valuable assistance in this venture, and was ever ready with sympathy and encouragement for those who intended adopting music as a profession – a fact to which I can testify from personal experience.

When Lloyd decided to leave Gloucester he wished me to accompany him and act as his assistant at Christ Church, as I had been at Gloucester. A church organistship in Oxford was vacant at the time, and I sent in my name as a candidate.[5] The vicar was satisfied with my credentials and offered me the post. This he did without consulting the churchwardens, who, on hearing of it, strongly objected. One reason, I discovered afterwards, was because a relative of one of the wardens was anxious to obtain the position. To satisfy the wardens the vicar decided to have a trial, the wardens choosing the adjudicator. I played Bach's *Prelude and Fugue in D major*[6] for my test piece, and I must confess felt satisfied with my performance. The other candidate (I should mention there were only two of us, the warden's relative and myself) played the 'Hallelujah Chorus' from the *Messiah*. It was difficult to recognize it, but it evidently satisfied the adjudicator and wardens, for my rival was appointed.

My failure to secure this post proved a blessing in disguise. Walter Parratt's promotion to Windsor from Magdalen College created a vacancy at St Giles's Church, a post he had held for some years with Magdalen.[7] After playing a service there in July, 1882, to the satisfaction of the vicar, the Reverend L. Sharpe,[8] the position

---

5   The church in question has not been identified.
6   BWV 532.
7   Sir Walter Parratt (1841–1924) was organist of Magdalen College, Oxford, from 1872 to 1882 and of St George's Chapel, Windsor Castle, from 1882 to 1924.
8   The Rev'd Lancelot Lambert Sharpe was Vicar of St Giles's Church from 1880 to 1884.

was offered to me. From every point of view it was a great advance on the church for which I had previously competed. The salary was larger, and, what was still more important, the standard of the music was on a much higher level, as can be readily imagined with so distinguished a musician at the head of it. I felt a little diffident about succeeding so brilliant an organist, but the encouragement and sympathy I received, and the confidence of youth, caused this feeling soon to wear off.

Three and a half years I spent in this church, and eventful years they were too, for it was during this period of my life that I made so many friends, whose friendship I valued and still value. H. B. Deane, a Fellow of St John's College,[9] who was vicar the latter part of the time, was a cultured musician and an expert violoncellist. He was a quaint character and very untidy in his dress, but the charm of his winning and sympathetic personality was irresistible. Much music was performed during his vicariate. Often on Sunday evenings he would gather together the best amateurs to play Handel's Organ Concertos and other pieces suitable for strings and organ at the close of the service.

In the early part of 1883 I competed successfully for the first open organ scholarship at the Royal College of Music, which had just been opened by the Prince of Wales (afterwards Edward VII). There I studied the organ with Sir Walter Parratt, composition with Sir Charles Stanford, counterpoint with Sir Frederick Bridge[10] and violoncello with Mr Edward Howell.[11] At the same time I carried out the duties at St Giles's Church in addition to acting as Lloyd's assistant at Christ Church Cathedral. I held this scholarship for only two terms, having successfully competed at the end of the Michaelmas term, 1883, for the organ scholarship at Exeter College. The journey to and fro several times during the week between Oxford and London proved too great a tax on my not over-robust

---

9   Henry B. Deane was Vicar of St Giles's Church, Oxford, from 1874 to 1880 and again from 1884 to 1887.

10 Bridge was Organist of Westminster Abbey from 1882 to 1918.

11 Edward Howell (1846–98) was Professor of 'Cello at the Royal Academy of Music and at the Guildhall School of Music, in addition to the Royal College of Music. The Scholars' Register at the Royal College of Music notes that Brewer also took lessons in Harmony with 'Barnett', presumably John Francis Barnett (1837–1916).

health and, for that reason, I did not regret the exchange of scholarship from the R.C.M. to Exeter College.[12]

Exeter College possessed a musical reputation: Dr Bridge[13] of Chester Cathedral, Mr Brooksbank[14] of Llandaff Cathedral, Mr Scotson Clark[15] of march fame had all held the organ scholarship; and Sir Hubert Parry, who had taken his Mus. Bac. degree at Oxford whilst still a boy at Eton, was an undergraduate of that College.

The then Rector of Exeter, Dr Lightfoot,[16] always reminded me of the man who said he knew two tunes; one was *God save the Queen* and the other wasn't. I remember on one occasion after an evening service (it was either the Queen's accession or her birthday) playing the National Anthem with variations as a voluntary. He recognized the tune when it was played over first, and remained standing in his place. But the first variation was rather complex and, thinking it was another piece, he made a move from his stall. He was getting infirm and moved slowly, so that by the time he was well out of his stall I began to play the second variation. Here the tune was clear and obvious, and he immediately stood at attention again. The third variation, being in a minor key, was beyond his grasp, so he continued walking to the door; but the fourth variation pulled him up again, and so it continued until the end of the piece, much to the annoyance of the dons and undergraduates, who were more interested in the dinner menu than organ music.[17]

---

12 The Royal College of Music Scholars' Register confirms that Brewer resigned his scholarship "on account of ill health".
13 Joseph Bridge (1853–1929) was the younger brother of Sir Frederick Bridge.
14 Hugh Brooksbank (1854–94), organist of Llandaff Cathedral from 1882 until his death.
15 The Rev'd Frederick Scotson Clark (1840–83) was a renowned composer of lacklustre marches for organ.
16 Dr John Prideaux Lightfoot (1803–87) was Rector of Exeter from 1854 until his death. He was Vice-Chancellor of Oxford University from 1862 to 1866.
17 Several organ works incorporate variations on the tune of the National Anthem. They include Johann Christian Heinrich Rinck's *Variationen 'Heil dir im Siegerkranz'* (from *Praktische Orgelschule*, Op.55), W. T. Best's *Introduction, Variations and Finale on 'God save the Queen'* (Op.29), Charles Ives's *Variations on 'America'* (1891) and Max Reger's *Variationen und Fuge über 'Heil unserem König Heil'* ('Heil dir im Siegerkranz') (1901). Brewer's description has some features in common with the compositions by Rinck and Best, though it does not fully accord with either.

In addition to carrying out the duties of organist and choirmaster I conducted the Musical Society in the College. We devoted all our energies to one concert in the summer term and performed many interesting choral works, accompanied by a professional London orchestra, which also contributed a symphony to the programme, thereby providing a rare treat for Oxford music lovers; a London orchestra, in those days, being an almost unheard-of luxury and pleasure in the provinces. The boys of the chapel choir, who were accustomed to sing a cathedral service on Saturdays, Sundays and Saints' days, took the treble and alto parts, and we relied on the undergraduates of the College to supply the tenor and bass parts.

It was at Oxford I first met Sir Frederick Ouseley,[18] at that time Professor of Music in the University. A more sympathetic and kind-hearted man never lived. There was always a warm welcome for his numerous friends at St Michael's College, Tenbury (of which he was the principal Founder and the Warden). But he disliked smoking, and had a strong objection to the smell of tobacco about the house. His guests therefore, when anxious to indulge in the soothing weed, adjourned to a neighbouring cottage, where lived a member of the choir, and there smoked and played whist till the early hours of the morning.

Ouseley was much attached to Spohr's music, and it always gave him immense pleasure to play that composer's Quartet in G minor,[19] arranged as a pianoforte duet. It was his custom carefully to remind the person who played the bass part (he took care never to let anyone but himself play the treble part) not to hurry the last movement. Of course, we all knew exactly what was going to happen; he set the pace at a moderate speed, but his excitement soon carried him away, and the pace became faster and faster until it reached a breakneck speed, and the result was nothing but a scramble. He appeared to be quite unconscious of being the delinquent. He prided himself on being able to sing the Litany without the book; but, as years advanced, his memory, at times, failed, and I recollect hearing

18 Sir Frederick Arthur Gore Ouseley, 2nd Baronet (1825–89). His principal service to English church music was his founding of St Michael's College, Tenbury, which was intended to serve as a model for the practice of Anglican church music, and which he personally endowed.

19 The String Quartet Op.4, No.2 in G minor had been published in an arrangement for four hands by August Schlums (Augener, n.d.).

him repeat a petition several times before he could remember what followed.

He always delighted in telling the story of a double bass player who had been sent to deputize for a professional man in a performance of Beethoven's Second Symphony at Tenbury. At the rehearsal not only was the professional man missing but the double bass part was nowhere to be found. The deputy, by no means nonplussed, asked Ouseley what key the symphony was in. On being told D major, he said, "I suppose D and A will do!" He was accustomed to play at quadrille parties. When Ouseley first went to Oxford in the early forties music was considered so effeminate that his request for permission to have a piano in his rooms surprised and astonished the College authorities. This astounding request was eventually granted on very strict conditions.

Another of my earliest friends in the University was (Sir) Henry Hadow,[20] at that time Dean of Worcester College. He occupied a prominent position in the musical life of Oxford. He studied composition with Lloyd, and many chamber works with original ideas were the result. One innovation – considered a remarkable one at that time – was a slow movement in a pianoforte sonata written in 21/8 time.[21] His memory is phenomenal. I have seen him, when asked to accompany a song he had not seen before, glance at it for a few minutes, holding the music close to his eyes on account of defective sight, then put the music aside and sit down and play it from memory.

When sending me one of his first publications – a beautiful setting of Shelley's words, *Music when soft voices die*[22] – he inscribed on the copy the following lines:

> If you want a reception that's bound to be truer
> Than gushes of critic or snarls of reviewer,
> I advise you, my song,
> To retire from the throng,
> And go knock at the door of Brewer, of Brewer.

---

20 William Henry Hadow (1859–1937) was a noted educational reformer and music historian. He was Vice-Chancellor of Durham (1916–19) and Sheffield (1919–30) universities.

21 This is almost certainly the Pianoforte Sonata in G sharp minor, published by Augener in about 1886.

22 Published by Ewer & Co. [1884].

So I summon you forth from Novello and Ewer
(He called himself E-wer, but my name is newer)
And bid you convey
As you hasten away
My compliments offered to Brewer, to Brewer.

W. H. H.

I have already referred to the University Musical Club which
Lloyd founded in 1871. This Society did much for the advancement of
chamber music in the University. It was, at one period, my privilege
to be President of the Club, an honour I greatly appreciated. We gave
weekly concerts on Tuesday evenings at the Club Rooms in the High,
and string players of worldwide reputation took part. I remember,
during my term of office, Joachim was engaged to perform, and
delighted everybody with his playing of Bach. He also produced at
the same concert a new violin sonata by Lloyd, whose guest he was
during his visit. After dinner that night I was asked to make a fourth
at whist, the party consisting of Joachim and his brother, Lloyd and
myself. Joachim had never played the game before and was much
mystified. Lloyd explained to him that if he wished to puzzle his
adversary he should trump his partner's trick, which advice he
obediently carried out!

But there sprang up a feeling amongst certain members of the
University that a Club should be formed and concerts given by the
members without professional assistance. This movement was the
outcome of Sunday evening "Smokers" at the house of the Reverend
J. H. Mee, the prime mover, and a most enthusiastic musician.[23]
The New Society – The Musical Union – was founded in 1884 and
held its meetings in a large room behind the shop occupied by Mr
Taphouse in the Cornmarket.[24]

I joined the Musical Union at its inception, and was elected to
serve on the first committee. I had hoped that the two Societies
would combine in their efforts to promote the advancement of music
in Oxford, and did everything in my power to bring this about; but

---

23   John Henry Mee (1852–1918). See p.25, fn.27.
24   The Taphouse family music shop traded at 3 Magdalen Street, Oxford, from 1859
     to 1982.

my efforts, unfortunately, were unavailing. In fact, the Musical Union was looked upon by *some* as an opposition society, and, in consequence, an amusing caricature appeared in Shrimpton's windows,[25] depicting a performance in the Broad, outside Balliol College, by the leading members of the Musical Union, interrupted by the arrival on the scene of members of the Musical Club, claiming the right of performance on that spot. The high standard of the performances of the Musical Club, in comparison with the efforts of the Musical Union, is amusingly portrayed in the titles on the music carried by their respective representatives – the present Bishop of Oxford[26] and myself. Since those days wiser counsels have prevailed. The two Societies, now amalgamated, hold their concerts in the Holywell Music Room. It is interesting to record that this Room, well known to many generations of undergraduates, was opened in 1748, and is the oldest Music Room in England.[27] For many years Malchair,[28] a prominent violinist in his day, gave concerts there. He also frequently played at the Gloucester Festivals from 1759 to 1775. Gloucester preserves a trace of him as a musician, one of the Cathedral chimes that are played daily having come from his pen.[29]

It will be seen that chamber music was well looked after in Oxford, and there was a flourishing orchestral society conducted by Lloyd; but choral singing was at a very low ebb, and great difficulty was found in keeping the Choral Society alive. One reason for this was probably the fact that nearly every College had its own Society.

In addition to conducting one in my own College, I was placed in charge of the Society at Merton. Hitherto the College Societies had been restricted to male voice choruses, for in those days women had not begun to assert their rights and the suffragist movement was undreamt of. The choice of music, in consequence, was very restricted, and I determined to make an effort to introduce ladies into the societies. Fortunately the proposal met with little opposition

---

25 Shrimpton's was an Oxford family business specialising in printing, bookbinding, picture-framing, etc., and was located at 20 Broad Street.
26 Thomas Banks Strong. See p.18, fn.4.
27 See John H. Mee, *The Oldest Music Room in Europe* (London, 1911).
28 Jean Baptist Malchair (= Johann Baptist Malscher, 1721–1812), German artist and musician, who lived in Oxford from 1759 to 1792.
29 For other Gloucester Cathedral chimes by Stephen Jeffries and John Stephens see pp.53 & 137 below.

from the dons, and the Merton Society was the first to give a concert at which ladies assisted. Their example was followed by Keble, and then other Colleges, with very satisfactory results.

It was at a concert given by Merton that I had my first experience in conducting an orchestra. The work performed was Schubert's *Unfinished Symphony*, and, at this same concert, my first song, written for and sung by Miss Beatrice Max Müller,[30] was produced. It was also at a Merton concert that we narrowly escaped a catastrophe. A London singer had been engaged to take the soprano part in Barnett's *Paradise and the Peri*. She was evidently a lady of much self-confidence, for she begged to be excused the rehearsal. This confidence I did not share, and insisted on her attendance. It was fortunate that I did, for the good lady arrived with a copy of Schumann's *Paradise and the Peri*. I also conducted the Society at Jesus College. Here the Welsh language gave me considerable trouble in correcting mistakes at the rehearsals.

Although secular choral music had been in a bad way, Lloyd accomplished much for sacred music. Not only did he raise the services at Christ Church to a much higher level, but he organized performances of Bach's *St Matthew Passion* and Spohr's *Last Judgement* and other works, which took place in the Cathedral. The chorus was drawn from Magdalen, New and Christ Church choirs. Lloyd conducted and I played. I gained much experience and derived some pleasure from conducting a Ladies' Society which met at various houses in the Parks, and which consisted chiefly of the wives and daughters of the dons. It was at one of these rehearsals, held at his house, that I had the pleasure of meeting Professor Max Müller.[31] It was the day following the death of the Emperor Frederick[32] – I well recall the occasion and the Professor saying that it would not be many years before the Kaiser Wilhelm[33] would be at war with

30 Beatrice Max Müller (d.1902) was the daughter of Professor (Friedrich) Max Müller (see fn.31 below).
31 Friedrich Max Müller (1823–1900), usually known as Max Müller, was successively Taylorian Professor of Modern European Languages, Professor of Comparative Philology, and the first Professor of Comparative Theology (1868–75) at Oxford.
32 Emperor Frederick III, King of Prussia and German Kaiser, died of cancer of the larynx on 15 June 1888.
33 Wilhelm II (1859–1941) was the last German Emperor and King of Prussia.

England. He evidently knew the temperament of the man who plunged the world into a state of chaos better than our politicians.

An amusing incident happened at Gloucester in connection with the Emperor Frederick's illness. When Europe was watching his struggle for life, and the papers were giving full details of his illness, the Dean of Gloucester, Dr Spence,[34] announced at an Organ Recital in the Cathedral that he had received from a person of high authority the news that the Emperor had passed away. He then asked the congregation to stand and to keep silence for three minutes, after which the organist, Lee Williams,[35] played the *Dead March in Saul*. The congregation awoke next morning to read in their papers that the Emperor had passed a good night and was better!

I remember seeing Ruskin[36] one day examining the title-pages of comic songs in Taphouse's shop window. He entered the shop and made a selection, his choice evidently not pleasing the assistant, who recommended something quite different as being better music. But Ruskin replied that it was not for the sake of the music that he had chosen those particular songs, but for the purpose of protesting against the vicious taste of the day in the drawing and colouring of the title-pages. A collection of title-pages was immediately made for him.

It was during my Oxford days, whilst assisting at a Festival at Fairford, that my fondness for a practical joke got the upper hand, and I perpetrated an unpardonable breach of good behaviour. Arthur Loxley, who had been a Minor Canon at Gloucester when I was a chorister, was vicar of Fairford at the time and conducted the performance. Professional instrumentalists were engaged from Oxford and elsewhere, and we all assembled in the church on the morning of the performance to rehearse. I gave B flat for the orchestra to tune to! The players could not understand the pitch. I heard them say that the A (which they imagined was the note I gave) was the highest they had ever experienced. The conductor gave them

---

34 From 1904 onwards Spence adopted the surname 'Spence-Jones' in accordance
    with the provisions of a family will (he had married Louisa Jones in 1871). See
    p.54, fn.9.
35 Charles Lee Williams (1853–1935), organist of Gloucester Cathedral from 1882 to
    1896, succeeded C. H. Lloyd.
36 John Ruskin (1819–1900), the versatile Victorian artist, critic, philanthropist and
    social thinker.

the signal to start. The hideous crash produced by the orchestra playing a semitone higher than the organ can be left to the reader's imagination. The conductor stopped the rehearsal and exclaimed, "Something is wrong!" It was hardly necessary to inform the players of the fact, for a more diabolical noise had never been heard before. It was some time before peace was restored. My mischievous prank caused some misgivings the next time I assisted at their Festival as to who was at fault when mistakes occurred.

As I have already stated, my reason for going to Oxford was to act as Lloyd's assistant, and to study music. The possession of a degree was not so essential to musicians then as now, and at the commencement of my sojourn there my whole time was devoted to studying music and also teaching it. Subsequently I worked with the intention of taking a degree, but the failure of my eyes and my general state of health prevented its accomplishment, and I left Oxford without an Arts degree. But I laid the foundation of many valuable friendships.

I left Oxford in December, 1885, and thought I was leaving the University city for good; but, as events turned out, my surmise proved wrong. On December 2nd the following poem appeared in the *Oxford Magazine*. The author was L. W. Lyde[37] of Queen's, who had previously written verses for me to set to Music:[38]

A SONNET – To A. H. B.

November 30th, 1885

Soft music steals athwart the evening air,
    And creeps from wall to roof, from roof to wall,
Leaving its trembling echoes everywhere
    To float awhile, then dreamily to fall.
But ever in the unhushed harmony
    More than a swelling chorus wooes my heart,
More than a glorious anthem 'tis to me,
    It is the prayer of those who fear to part.

---

37 Lionel William Lyde (1863–1947) was to become Professor of Geography at the University of London from 1903 to 1928.

38 *The Lover's Hour* (Taphouse and Son, [1885]) and *The Power of Night* (Hutchings and Co., [1885]).

And through the mingled notes of praise one song,
  Low, sad and tender, comes – and comes from thee,
Breaking the happy memories, which throng,
  Of what has been, henceforward, not to be.
My friend, my best beloved, thou art gone!
  The chords are silent, and I am alone.

                                        L. W. L.

− 4 −

Bristol/Oxford (1885–6)

George Riseley[1] was appointed organist of Bristol Cathedral in 1876, and was sworn in under the statutes governing the Cathedral. Subsequently disputes arose between him and the Precentor[2] concerning the musical services. On one occasion the latter gave instructions that a certain anthem should be sung; but Riseley, considering that the choir, in consequence of the absence of two of the principal singers, could not render it adequately, substituted another. The Precentor complained to the Chapter, and, after some correspondence, the Dean and Chapter, imagining that they had full control over the position, gave Riseley three months' notice to quit.

When thinking of becoming a candidate for the post, I consulted my old friend, Sir Frederick Ouseley, and received from him the following letter:

Tenbury,
July 5th, 1885.

My dear Brewer

I believe Mr Riseley is going to law with the Dean and Chapter of Bristol about the organistship. But still it may be worth your while to go in for it, so I will write a strong letter in your favour to Archdeacon Norris,[3] and Canon Wade,[4] whom I know well, and that will be far better than

---

1   For an account of George Riseley (1845–1932) see Shaw, *The Succession of Organists*, pp.40–41. A full discussion of Riseley's dispute with the Dean and Chapter is given in Edmund H. Fellowes, *Memoirs of an Amateur Musician* (London, 1946), pp.74–7.
2   The Rev'd Canon William James Mann was Precentor from 1882 to 1897. His inflexibility concerning the authority of the Precentor in all musical matters was notorious.
3   The Rev'd Canon John Pilkington Norris (1823–91) was Archdeacon from 1881 to 1891.
4   The Rev'd Canon Nugent Wade (1809–93) was Rector of St Anne, Soho, from 1846 to 1890, and concurrently Canon of Bristol Cathedral from 1872.

any testimonial. I'll do it by to-day's post. I am sorry to hear you have been so seedy – *very sorry.*

> Yours most sincerely
> Frederick A. G. Ouseley

I was also strongly supported in my application by Lloyd and Sir Walter Parratt, and was duly appointed. But before taking up the work at Bristol I received the following letter from the Dean:

> Clifton
> Nov. 16th, 1885

Dear Sir

Canon Percival[5] forwarded to me an account of a conversation which he has had with you. I am ready to appoint you formally to fill the office of Organist in this Cathedral from the earliest date you can undertake its duties at a salary of £150 a year, but on these conditions, that in case Mr Riseley succeeds in his contention, your engagement made with the Chapter shall be held to be determined, that in case we shall have to forego your services, you are to receive a proportionate amount of £150, comparing the time you have served with a year, that further the Chapter will give you three months additional salary from the date of your leaving to close your services, by reason of Mr Riseley's return. May I beg early information whether you accept these terms, and may I also hope that if you do you will be able to commence your duties early in December.

> Yours faithfully
> Gilbert Elliott[6]

I accepted these conditions and took up my abode in Bristol in December, 1885. The case came before Mr Jeune (afterwards

---

5 Canon John Percival (1834–1918) held many prestigious appointments, including President of Trinity College, Oxford (1878–87), Headmaster of Rugby School (1887–95) and Bishop of Hereford (1895–1917).
6 The Very Rev'd Gilbert Elliott (1800–91) was Dean of Bristol from 1850 until his death.

Lord St Helier),[7] Chancellor of the Diocese. Mr Riseley, through Mr Charles, QC, contended that the Dean and Chapter were acting illegally, and that being on the foundation of the Cathedral he could not be removed in the way he had been. That could only be done for a very grave offence, and then only after three admonitions.

Sir Walter Phillimore,[8] who represented the capitular body, submitted that Mr Riseley's act and letters amounted to insubordination, and that the Dean and Chapter were acting within their rights in removing him. The Chancellor, upholding Mr Riseley's claim, said he must be reinstated in his position.

The Bristol *Times and Mirror*, in a leading article on the case on January 27th 1886, said:

> Judgment was given in the Riseley case yesterday, and, as nearly everybody, save the Dean and Chapter, expected, it was in favour of the appellant, who has been reinstated in his position as Organist at the Cathedral. As his dismissal is thus held to be illegal, Mr Riseley's long connection with the Cathedral, extending over a generation, remains unbroken, and may possibly last for another generation to the mutual advantage of both Church and Organist. Perhaps the surest way of securing peace would be to make Mr Riseley Precentor as well as Organist. As this cannot be, there must be a mutual understanding as to the rights and duties of those holding the different offices. This is all the more necessary, because the Chancellor declined to say whether the Precentor or the Organist was in fault in the matter which directly led to the rupture. That there is a disposition to arrange matters amicably is proved by the readiness with which the parties to the recent action have, presumably, shaken hands, by arranging that no unseemly wrangle shall follow the resumption by Mr Riseley of his position in the organ-loft.
>
> Satisfaction at Mr Riseley's success will be tempered with regret at the unfortunate position with which Mr

---

7   Mr (later Sir) Francis Jeune (1843–1905), 1st Baron St Helier, was President of the Probate, Divorce and Admiralty Division of the High Court from 1891 until 1905. His father, The Rt Rev'd Francis Jeune (1806–68) was Bishop of Peterborough from 1864 until his death.

8   Sir Walter (later Lord) Phillimore (1845–1929) was a Judge of the Queen's Bench Division of the High Court (1897–1913) and Lord Justice of Appeal (1913–16).

Brewer finds himself. But of course the Dean and Chapter, to whom this is due, will take care that he does not suffer; while his undoubted abilities are certain to secure for him a position at least as important and lucrative as that which he will now, it is presumed, have to surrender.

I have dwelt at length on the case because the position of Precentor and organist is one to which I have given much thought, and to which (this is a point I would emphasize strongly) the authorities in our Cathedrals might give, with great advantage, their careful consideration. The suggestion made in the *Times and Mirror* that Mr Riseley should be made Precentor as well as organist was a sound one. Mr Riseley is not the only organist who has fallen foul of his Precentor. It was the young Precentor with little knowledge of music who caused so much unhappiness in Wesley's life. The office of Precentor is usually held by a Minor Canon. He is, generally speaking, a young man who has recently been ordained, and is, as is natural at that age, rather full of his own ideas. He possesses little real knowledge of music and is only an amateur in the art. Contrast with that the position of organist. The organist has made music his life's study, and has attained his position by virtue of his musical gifts and ability, and is a man high up in his profession. It will readily be seen how unwise it is to entrust the choice and control of the music to the amateur in preference to the musical expert.

The unfortunate, though not wholly unexpected, position I was placed in, as the result of Mr Riseley's reinstatement, brought me many letters of sympathy, amongst which was one from the well-known novelist, Emma Marshall, who had lived in Gloucester during my chorister days, and was then living at Clifton.[9] She wrote:

Woodside
Leigh Woods, Clifton
January 27, 1886

I am indeed *very* sorry. I never anticipated this result of the trial! I thought Riseley would clear himself, but never imagined he would go back to the Cathedral.

9   Emma Marshall (1830–99) was a prolific novelist, many of whose works are historical in nature.

You are a great loss *here* but I feel sure better things
are ready for you. This is not an inviting Cathedral nor are
"the powers that be" in unity with each other. So in that
respect you have lost nothing. Still I know all the worry
and anxiety you have had, and you ought not to have been
brought here on any uncertainty.

We shall hear of you at the top of the tree somewhere,
of that there can be little doubt.

With kind regards and good wishes,

Yours very truly
Emma Marshall

It is recorded that, on the day of Riseley's re-appearance at the
Cathedral, the anthem was *How dear are Thy Counsels* (Crotch),
and as a Voluntary he played *Fixed in His Everlasting Seat*
(Handel)![10] The Dean, so report said, had not attended a cathedral
service for ten years until I took up the duties of organist. Whether
this was an accurate statement or not, I cannot say; but it is quite
possible, for the friction began some years before the case came to
a head.

I cannot close the account of my association with Bristol without
referring to the Madrigal Society which was founded as far back
as 1837, and was conducted by D. W. Rootham.[11] It was during my
brief residence in the western city that I renewed my acquaintance
with this Society and its excellent work. As a boy I had taken part in
more than one of their concerts. In those days the Society engaged
the services of men and boys from some of the principal cathedrals
and college choirs in England to take part in their concerts. It was
an event the Gloucester boys looked forward to with delight. At
least four incidents connected with these functions made lasting
impressions on my boyish memory: the music, which gave me
immense pleasure, the style so closely resembling Byrd and Gibbons
and other writers of that period which I loved; the sights of Clifton
and Bristol, not forgetting the Zoo; the wearing of white kid gloves

---

10 The final chorus of Handel's oratorio *Samson*.
11 Daniel Wilberforce Rootham (1837–1922), a pupil of Thomas Attwood Walmisley,
    was a prominent Bristol musician. His son, Cyril F. Rootham, was organist of St
    John's College, Cambridge, from 1901 to 1938.

– probably my first appearance in such finery; and last, but by no means least, that which would appeal to most boys of tender age and robust appetite, the luscious cherry tarts at the Queen's Hotel, where we stayed during our short holiday.

I well recollect sitting side-by-side with Hubert Hunt, who was then a chorister at Windsor and who is now organist of the Cathedral at Bristol and conducts the Madrigal Society.[12]

When the time arrived for me to leave Bristol I returned to Oxford, the Rector and Fellows of Exeter College having most generously offered to renew my organ scholarship. I should mention that it had been held in abeyance as the College authorities were aware of the conditions under which I took up the post at Bristol Cathedral. In the meantime F. C. Woods[13] had been acting as organist; and in the following autumn, when I gave up all thoughts of remaining in Oxford, he was elected organ scholar in my place. He was not only a skilled performer on the organ, but was also a past-master at playing practical jokes. Many a fresher had cause to remember F.C.W.

---

12 Hubert Walter Hunt (1865–1945) was organist of Bristol Cathedral from 1901 until his death.

13 Francis Cunningham Woods (1862–1929) was organist of Brasenose College (1883–6), and of Exeter College from 1886 to 1895. He was a composition pupil of Sir Arthur Sullivan.

− 5 −

Coventry (1886–92)

When I finally left Oxford it was to take up my residence in Coventry, the city with the beautiful cluster of three spires and of Peeping Tom fame.[1] I had been appointed organist of St Michael's, that vast church, which Sir Christopher Wren declared to be a masterpiece in the art of Gothic building, and the steeple of which was an ideal structure in Ruskin's eyes. It is one of the largest parish churches in England and dates from 1350. At the time of my appointment it was being restored at a cost of some £40,000. This great work the authorities were able to carry out through the munificence of a local solicitor, Mr George Woodcock,[2] who not only contributed the greater part of this sum, but also provided a further amount to defray the cost of a new organ. The building had been in urgent need of repair; the method of ventilating the church was through openings in or near the roof, through which birds flew in and out causing much annoyance to the worshippers. Old residents of Coventry used to tell me of a former vicar who was in the habit of going into the church on a Monday morning and, taking up his position at the east end, would shoot the birds as they came through these openings.

When the roof was being restored I climbed the scaffolding and saw holes in the oak which certainly might have been caused by the pellets from the gun of this extraordinary individual, who chose this unseemly method of satisfying his sporting instincts. Hitherto the organ had been supported on pillars at the west end of the church

---

1   According to legend, Lady Godiva's naked ride on horseback through the streets of Coventry was witnessed by 'Peeping Tom', in breach of an undertaking by the townspeople not to gaze at her, hence the use of the term 'Peeping Tom' to describe a voyeur. Brewer was organist of St Michael's from 1886 to 1892. St Michael's was designated as the cathedral on the establishment of the Coventry diocese in 1918. It was destroyed by enemy bombing on the night of 14 November 1940.
2   George Woodcock (1838–91) was a prominent local businessman. He owned the King's Head Hotel, and had many diverse business interests.

with a large gallery for the singers, but at the restoration both were removed. The choir had been a mixed one – ladies supplied the soprano and alto parts, with a sprinkling of boys to sing treble.

The order for the new instrument was given to Henry Willis,[3] who then had the building and re-building of most of the principal organs in the country. The church authorities had little idea of the length of time required to construct an organ, and imagined that a few weeks would suffice. The time drew near for the reopening of the church, but the Coventry organ had made little progress in Willis's factory. It was during this period that the famous builder was erecting one for the new cathedral at Truro, which building was in such an unfinished state that it was decided to delay placing the organ there until a later date. In consequence of this the Coventry church received the instrument originally intended for Truro.

When I entered on my duties at the end of September, 1886, I was given a very hearty welcome by the civic and church authorities, who entertained me at dinner – an unusual honour for a church organist! In the members of the Vestry I found a body of sympathetic men who readily supported me in all my enterprises. One of the first of these was to form a choir consisting of men and boys only, without the assistance of ladies. This was successfully carried through, and within a few weeks I had a choir of some forty boys and twenty-four men. What was even a greater innovation was the fact that all the members were voluntary. This was the first time a purely voluntary choir was formed in Coventry. The movement caused some consternation amongst the church choirs, as hitherto all members had received some remuneration. But, in spite of this, the example set by St Michael's was soon followed by the other churches, and the standard of singing generally rapidly rose to a much higher level. We did a cathedral service on Sundays, the only day in the week when a full choir attended, and, by so doing, prepared the way for those who presided over the music when the church became a cathedral.

The reopening of St Michael's Church took place on Easter Sunday, 1887, when the organ was used for the first time. It was then, as it is now, unadorned by a case. The funds available were limited, and the Vestry, acting on my advice, put all the money 'inside'.

---

3   Henry Willis (1821–1901) is usually described as 'Father' Willis to distinguish him from later members of this family firm of organ builders.

The absence of a case gave rise to an amusing incident. Owen,[4] the verger, was approached by a stranger thirsting for knowledge with regard to the church, and as they drew near the organ the stranger looked up and said: "I don't think much of your organ." I imagine he meant the appearance of it, as he had not heard it speak. He went on to say that he was a bit of a judge, as his father used to play the harmonium in their village church! He then asked the name of the organist, and, on being told, declared he had never heard of me. This rather nettled Owen, who firmly believed in me, and he indignantly retorted: "What! Never heard of him? Why he took the gold medal at the Pedalling Exhibition in London last year!" "He *must* be good," exclaimed the stranger, completely dumbfounded.

Owen was a character and full of repartee. In his youth he had been a bus conductor in London, and no doubt had had his wits sharpened in this capacity. Few people scored off him. It was after I had left Coventry in 1892, when, on a return visit to the city, I was playing in St Michael's late one night, that Owen came in and asked me if I was not afraid to play in the dark. "No, why should I be?" I replied. "I have done it dozens of times before." "Then you haven't heard what happened here four nights ago?" He then related to me the following remarkable occurrence. A well-known citizen, one of the vestrymen, had died, and the choir was rehearsing on the Friday night the music for the funeral service, which was to take place the next day. The church was in darkness, save for the gas lights in the chancel, where the choir was assembled. Owen was standing with his son, at the extreme east end of the church, when suddenly his son shouted, "Look, father, look at this thing coming up the church." On looking down he saw a grey figure coming up the south side carrying what appeared to be a lighted lamp. The figure passed through the centre pews of the nave and went to the seat which the deceased gentleman had been in the habit of occupying. Owen immediately rushed to the spot, but found the pew empty.

In the meantime the boys of the choir, thoroughly scared, bolted out of the church through the vestry door, which was at the east end. Owen, still thinking it was someone playing a practical joke, proceeded with some of the senior members of the choir to search

---

4   John Parker Owen (1828–1913).

the church. They had not gone very far when they saw the same figure again move slowly across the west end of the building and disappear *through* a wooden structure, which had been erected in the north aisle as a screen for the bells (the bells had been removed from the tower during its restoration). This time some of the men fell down in sheer fright, but Owen, who was not so easily scared, made a dash for the wooden fence, which stood about seven feet from the ground, and climbed over and made a thorough search, but found nothing. Some suggested the apparition was caused by reflection from lamps outside the church, so experiments were made to try and solve the mystery, but without success. Whether the grey figure with the lamp has visited the church since I cannot say. Strange to relate the next day when the hearse approached the residence of the deceased vestryman, the horses jibbed, and absolutely refused to go near the house, and they had to be taken back to the stables and a fresh pair of horses used in their place.

When I first went to Coventry a performance of Sullivan's *Cox and Box* and *Trial by Jury* in aid of the funds of the old Musical Society was in contemplation. The latter work had been in preparation before the principal characters had been chosen. When the time came for the selection of these, a counsel for the plaintiff could not be found and, never caring to see one of the opposite sex in distress, I volunteered to plead her cause in Court. Having committed myself so far, I had to consent to take the part of Cox in the shorter work, and so I made my debut behind the footlights. *Cox and Box* became an instantaneous success, and we were in much request for performances in the Black Country in aid of various charities.

Music had developed in an extraordinary manner in many of the villages round Coventry. In these outlying districts enthusiastic amateurs were to be found who had high ideals in the art, and endeavoured to live up to them. This was especially noticeable in chamber music. It was no uncommon thing to hear a Beethoven or Schubert Trio or a String Quartet at an afternoon tea-party in these quiet villages and hamlets.

I cannot refrain from alluding to the vicar of one of these villages, an exceedingly quaint individual, who had the unfortunate knack of saying and doing the wrong thing. Some of the youthful members of his congregation caused him much trouble by their behaviour. They sat immediately below the pulpit, and when they considered the sermon should end they all with one accord pulled out their watches and, after looking at them, snapped their cases with a loud click. As a rule their action succeeded in bringing the sermon to an end. The vicar endured the disturbance for some time, but finally decided to speak to the congregation about their behaviour. He began by complaining of the way the services were conducted in the church, and added that he considered it a positive disgrace!

The path leading to his vicarage had become a moss-covered walk, and he lamented its condition to his chief parishioners. "But, unfortunately," he added, "I have not the means wherewith to purchase the gravel." On rising very early one morning he saw, to his great surprise, a load of gravel deposited in the road outside his gate. Thinking that Providence had heard his petition and supplied his need, he immediately, with the aid of his garden-boy, wheeled it into his garden, and before breakfast it had all disappeared from the road. A little later in the day, Mr R——m, who lived on the opposite side of the road, began to look about for the gravel which he had ordered for *his* drive. The scene can easily be imagined when he discovered the vicar in his shirt-sleeves, rolling it into the vicarage path.

The first two years or so of my life in Coventry were indeed happy ones: everything worked smoothly and flourished at St Michael's. On Bank Holiday afternoons I gave organ recitals which were supported by large congregations and which, I am glad to say, my successors have carried on; the Musical Society, which I conducted, gave performances of sacred works with great success in the church. But after a time some members of the Vestry, which was known as a close one, became discontented. They had now what they chose to call a new church, a new choir, a new organ and a new organist. To make it quite complete they wanted a new vicar. They thereupon began urging the vicar, Mr Butter,[5] to make an exchange, giving as their reason the fact that his health was not good, and that he would benefit by taking a lighter living.

An exchange was made, but the agitators soon discovered that they were out of the frying-pan into the fire. Everything went wrong

---

5　James Butter was Vicar of St Michael's from 1879 to 1888.

from that moment, and the culminating point was reached on Ascension Day, 1892. Part of the vicar's stipend came from a vicar's rate on the parish. The vicar strongly objected to his income coming from this source, and tried to compel the Vestry to raise it by other means. This they refused to do. In the meantime he had advised the parishioners not to pay the rate, hoping, by so doing, to force the hands of the Vestry. But in this he made a mistake, and it did not take him long to discover that he was the sufferer through his own action – his income being considerably reduced. He immediately veered round and instructed his solicitor to prosecute those who had not paid the vicar's rate. Those of his parishioners who refused to pay had their goods distrained, and an attempt was made to sell them by auction on Ascension Day, but without success, the unfortunate auctioneer being pelted with rotten eggs and other objectionable missiles. There was naturally a good deal of excitement about it in the city.

On his way to service that night the vicar was espied by an angry crowd which immediately gave chase. The vicar, a fat little man, who ran as fast as his short legs would allow, managed to reach the church and bolt the door just as the crowd was close on his heels. The noise of the crowd, which had now grown to an enormous size, was so deafening during the service that I could scarcely drown it with the organ, and there was great difficulty in leaving the church at the close of the service.

The *Coventry Mercury*, in giving an account of the day's proceedings, goes on to say:

> Mr. Brewer gallantly consented to take charge of the ladies of the congregation and he took them out by the vestry without hindrance. Next the boys made their escape from the beleaguered church. The Vicar and Junior Verger alone now remained inside, and the reader can understand the pacings to and fro of the Vicar, and his peerings through the windows at the mob thirsting for him. The shades of evening at last fell and now it was a curate reappeared at the vestry door with a supply of food. He knocked in vain, however, and could not get into the church. The Vicar, at last tired out, laid him down to sleep (he says) but his slumbers could hardly have been blissful. Towards eleven o'clock the crowd wore away, and the hour of the prisoner's

release was approaching. Then a friendly policeman
tapped gently at the avenue door, gave a signal, and Vicar
and Verger stepped out into the night. By a circuitous route
they reached the backdoor of the Vicarage. No doubt that
was a moment of relief to the Vicar and his friends.

This kind of excitement was more than I could stand, and I
determined, at the first opportunity, to seek pastures new. I had not
long to wait before I had the offer of two posts at the same time:
one at Bangor Cathedral, and the other at Tonbridge School, as
organist and music master. The attractions at the latter post were
many, and I decided to accept it.[6] Before taking leave of Coventry[7]
I cannot refrain from paying tribute to the unbounded musical
support I received from my many Coventry friends, amongst whom
stand out to a particular degree Dr and Mrs Pickup, who were ever
ready to organize, participate in, and financially assist any musical
project I contemplated. For many years before the war Dr Pickup
organized, under great difficulties for lack of a suitable building,
orchestral concerts. He was ably supported by his wife, who played
viola, his two sons, both young medical men, one an exceptionally
gifted 'cellist who lost his life during the war; and his daughter, Miss
Muriel Pickup, a brilliant violinist who was engaged as one of the
solo violinists at the Gloucester Festival in 1910.

I gained, in fact, so many true friends during my six years in the
city of spires that I never regretted being 'sent to Coventry'.

---

6   The vacant position at Bangor Cathedral was eventually taken by Tom Westlake
    Morgan (1869–1934), who held it until 1906.
7   September, 1892.

– 6 –
Tonbridge (1892–6)

My work at Tonbridge was entirely different from anything I had previously undertaken. The attempt to obtain good results from boys who naturally preferred cricket and football to irksome but necessary piano practice was a somewhat disheartening task. There was, however, compensation in the delightful companionship of the masters on the staff, many of whom I had known at Oxford. One of them – W. W. Rashleigh,[1] the famous Kent cricketer and a double Blue at Oxford – was a very helpful tenor in the choir, and no company could be dull which had for one of its members a soul so brimming over with fun and humour as A. H. Sharman, who on leaving Tonbridge became headmaster of the Khedive School in Cairo and subsequently lost his life in attempting to rescue a drowning friend whilst bathing. His merry, twinkling eye and infectious laugh were irresistible, and banished all feelings of despondency.

Another compensation was the generous support I received from the headmaster, Dr Wood,[2] who was one of the few headmasters of that time who understood the value of music as part of a boy's education, and who gave me a free rein to carry out my ideas. He allowed the boys to have their music lessons and attend choir practices during school hours, and he made a point of impressing on the boys' minds the privilege of singing in the choir. He also granted special favours to the members of the choir, not only by entertaining them in a lavish manner – as he knew how – but by giving them extra half-holidays during the term. When at all possible, I invited the boys who were prominent in the school – the Captains of the football and

---

1   William Rashleigh (1867–1937) played for Kent from 1885 to 1901 and for Oxford University from 1886 to 1889. While a schoolboy at Tonbridge he scored 203 against Dulwich.

2   The Rev'd Dr Joseph Wood (1842–1921), Headmaster of Tonbridge (1890–98) and of Harrow School (1898–1910), and subsequently Canon Residentiary of Rochester Cathedral.

cricket teams – to join the choir. This had an extraordinary effect in promoting musical ambition in the minds of the small boys, who looked up with awe and reverence to their athletic heroes.

Dr Wood also helped to improve the chapel services by giving choral scholarships. One of these scholars – Royal-Dawson by name[3] – had an extraordinarily beautiful treble voice. With him as solo boy I was able to perform such compositions as Wesley's *Wilderness*, selections from Dvořák's *Stabat Mater*, etc., at our chapel services, the tenor and bass parts being sung by masters – some of whom were worthy of a place in any choir – and several of the older boys in the school.

We were not so fortunate with our school chaplains. One of them imagined that the art of reading was to get through as many sentences as possible without taking breath. It happened on a Palm Sunday that he had to read the Gospel – the longest in the year – and he filled his lungs with a deep breath, which carried him through several lines, and then paused to take breath for a second effort. My thoughts on that occasion were far away (I had just become engaged) and, being suddenly conscious of the pause, I imagined the Gospel had come to an end and hastily started to play the Creed. I realized immediately my mistake, but, having always made it a rule not to turn back, I stuck to the note until the congregation took it up. On leaving the chapel at the close of the service I found all the masters assembled outside waiting to shake me warmly by the hand, and to tender their thanks for the abbreviated form of service!

The fame of the choir had spread beyond the town of Tonbridge, and we were invited by the Dean and Chapter of Canterbury to give a performance of a sacred work in Canterbury Cathedral, a privilege and an outing we all thoroughly enjoyed. As a result of this performance Dean Farrar[4] offered me the post of organist of the Cathedral when Dr Longhurst[5] contemplated retiring on a pension.

---

3   (Sir) Vernon Royal-Dawson KCIE (1881–1958) was at Tonbridge from 1893 to 1894, before transferring to St Paul's School. He served with the Indian (and later British) Civil Service as Under-Secretary to the Government of Bengal and East Assam. He was known in adulthood as Sir Vernon Dawson.
4   The Very Rev'd Frederick William Farrar (1831–1903), Dean of Canterbury from 1895 until his death.
5   William Henry Longhurst (1819–1904), organist of Canterbury Cathedral from 1873 to 1898.

He wished me to combine the Canterbury duties with my work at Tonbridge with the help of an assistant; but this was found to be quite impracticable, and all thought of such an arrangement had to be abandoned. When Dr Longhurst died I had already moved to Gloucester. Dr Wood was a man of imposing presence, with a singularly charming personality. Few could resist his winning manner, and the numbers in the School went up by leaps and bounds during his headmastership. There were one hundred and fifty boys in the school when he was appointed, and that number had been trebled when he left to become headmaster of Harrow. He was a wonderful reader of character, and was rarely at fault in selecting his assistant masters, and having appointed them he wisely left them to carry out their duties without interfering with them in any way.

He was inclined to be nervous about his health, and would remain in bed whenever he had the slightest suspicion of a cold; to nip it in the bud, as he was wont to say. He was not musical, but had often dry comments to make on the performance of music, and I recollect one occasion when he made use of music to give vent to his feelings. It was on a Sunday morning during service; he sent a pencilled note across the Chapel to ask me to play the 'Hallelujah Chorus' as a voluntary. I sent a message back to say that I had not got a copy of the *Messiah* with me, but I would do my best to play it from memory. At the close of the service I proceeded to carry out his request, and he came and stood by me. This was the first occasion on which he had asked me to play a special piece, and I wondered what the reason might be. I had not long to wait to have my curiosity satisfied, for as soon as I had finished playing he dug me in the ribs with his elbow and, with a chuckle of delight, exclaimed: "You know why I asked you to play that – Harcourt's kicked out!" The news had reached Tonbridge that morning that Sir William Harcourt had been defeated at Derby.[6]

Owing to the rapid growth of the School a temporary wooden and iron structure had been erected for use as a Chapel until funds should be forthcoming for the erection of a building worthy of its purpose and the School. (The old Chapel had long since become

---

6   William Vernon Harcourt (1827–1904), a prominent Liberal statesman, was
     defeated at the 1895 General Election.

inadequate, and had been utilized as a Museum.) It was in this makeshift place – very cold, damp and draughty in the winter and overwhelmingly hot in the summer – that I carried out my duties during the four and a half years I remained in Tonbridge. The sudden atmospheric changes had a bad effect on the organ, and often caused it to cipher; so much so, that, when I had finished the service, the blower, a poor, half-witted fellow, would go on pumping the wind in for some time, thinking that I was still playing! He was a quaint character, and amused me one day by requesting that he might be supplied with a psalter as he thought it would enable him to blow the psalms so much better!

In order to accommodate the increasing influx of boys new buildings on an extensive scale were being added. These included a new 'Big School' – a room which would seat a considerable number of people beyond the boys and masters. The architect had not considered the erection of an organ, but had planned a capital orchestra; and above this, at my request, he designed a recess for an organ. I then appealed to the Governors of the school for an organ, and, at their invitation, attended a meeting in London to advise them in the matter. I recommended that the order should be placed with Henry Willis, and asked for the sum of £1,000 – a considerable amount in those days – to be spent on the instrument. I had great difficulty in impressing on those city magnates the advantage of having a well-built and really fine instrument. One member remarked: "But surely, Mr Brewer, you could get an organ loud enough for the room for £100?" "No doubt," I replied, "you could get a steam organ loud enough which would not only *fill* the room, but *empty* it as well." They eventually consented when they realized that I should not be satisfied with less than £1,000, and it was to be that or nothing at all.

The order was placed with Willis, and the result was a perfectly voiced instrument of three manuals. The possession of such an organ made it possible to give recitals to the boys. By these means I was able to make them acquainted with a quantity of modern music as well as the old classics by transcribing them for the organ. To the majority of them Wagner was unknown, and the Overture to *Tannhäuser* became a great favourite. How different was their reception of it compared with that of the musical critic of *The Times* at its first performance in London on May 3rd, 1854! It was played at a Philharmonic Concert in St Martin's Hall and conducted by Dr Wylde.[7] The critic[8] writes:

> The almost impossible Overture of Herr Richard Wagner, introduced for the first time to an English audience, and played with surprising accuracy and decision, would do very well for a pantomime or Easter piece. It is a weak parody of the worst compositions, not of M. Berlioz, but of his imitators. So much fuss about nothing, such a pompous and empty commonplace has seldom been heard.

The musical representative of *The Times* was not the only one who took exception to this Overture. Joseph Bennett[9] – for many years musical critic of *The Daily Telegraph* – when writing about Sterndale Bennett, says:

> He had a pretty wit on occasion. When listening to the *Tannhäuser* Overture at Hanover Square Rooms in 1855, Wagner himself conducting, he exclaimed to some friends near at hand, "Why, this is Brummagem[10] Berlioz!" There could not have been a more apt and pithy expression of the feeling of the time with regard to Wagner and his music.

In addition to the recitals, singers and instrumentalists were engaged by Dr Wood to give concerts to the boys, so they were thoroughly steeped in music. There were also House Singing Classes once a week, with House Competitions at the end of the year. For use at these 'Sing-Songs' I collaborated with various masters in writing School Songs, and the *Football Song*, by A. H. Sharman, is still I believe most popular.[11] At the same time I founded a Choral Society in the town, and the concerts were also held in the 'Big School' by

---

7   Henry Wylde (1822–90), Gresham Professor of Music from 1863 to 1890, was one of the founders of the New Philharmonic Society (1852). St Martin's Hall, which opened in 1850, was located in Covent Garden. It became the Queen's Theatre in 1867.

8   James William Davison (1813–85), music critic for *The Times* from 1846 to 1885.

9   Gloucestershire-born Joseph Bennett (1831–1911) was music critic for *The Sunday Times* from 1865 to 1870 and for *The Daily Telegraph* from 1870 to 1906. He was also a well-known librettist.

10   i.e. from Birmingham ('Brum'), implying showy but of little artistic merit.

11   Published by Mathias and Strickland, n.d. [1893].

the courtesy of Dr Wood. Composer–conductors were invited to conduct their works, and Sir Frederick Bridge and Dr C. H. Lloyd were amongst the guest composers who came.

The music at the Parish Church was at a very low ebb, and an appeal was made to me for assistance. One of the churchwardens, a great lover of music but without knowledge of it, came to me in despair and urged me to remonstrate with the vicar about his choice of unmusical curates. He went on to say, "If the organist gives him (the curate) a note on which to intone he takes one two *bars* below!" One member of the Parish Church choir – a very little man with a very big bass voice – was not only an enthusiastic musician but a keen footballer. He would journey with the Tonbridge football team no matter how far they went. When returning from a match, in which some of the masters from the School had taken part, the little bass was discoursing on his experiences at the Chicago Exhibition. He went on to say how he had heard a singer with a wonderful bass voice, but he could not remember his name. Various singers of note were mentioned by my friends unsuccessfully. One member of the team, a bricklayer by trade, sitting in the corner of the carriage had been unsuccessfully endeavouring to join in the conversation. He now felt that this was his opportunity to let them see that *he* knew something about music, and, leaning forward, he said, "Was it 'Andel?"

It was at Tonbridge in 1896 that I had a curious experience. The organistship at Liverpool Town Hall became vacant through the resignation of W. T. Best.[12] I applied, and was chosen with two others to compete, one being Dr Peace,[13] who was eventually appointed. After hearing that I had been selected I dreamt most vividly that my friend, Lee Williams, was retiring from the organistship of Gloucester Cathedral, the post of all others which I wished to hold. The dream occurred on three successive nights and so unsettled me that I wrote to Liverpool to request that my name might be withdrawn from the list. On hearing of this my friends told me that

---

12 William Thomas Best (1826–97) was arguably the finest organist of his day. He inaugurated the organ at the Royal Albert Hall in 1871.
13 Albert Lister Peace (1844–1912) performed at the inauguration of many important organs, included those at Crystal Palace (1882), Canterbury Cathedral (1886) and Westminster Abbey (1909).

they considered my action extremely foolish, and urged me not to withdraw from the competition. The real reason of my withdrawal was not disclosed to them. On finding that they were distressed about it, and thinking that I had been unwise, I wired to the Town Clerk of Liverpool asking to be allowed to withdraw my letter of resignation. A telegram came in reply to say that another candidate's name had been inserted in place of mine, but the matter would come before a special committee the following day. The committee met, and decided to allow me to withdraw my letter.

Once again I had the same dream even more vividly. It had such a curious effect on me that I wired immediately to the Town Clerk begging that my name should be removed from the list. The reply from him was concise and to the point – "Have definitely withdrawn your name." That was the end of the Liverpool affair so far as I was concerned. A month later the organistship of Gloucester Cathedral became vacant through the resignation of Lee Williams on account of ill-health![14]

When the time came for my departure from Tonbridge I was much touched by the generous gifts that were showered on me from all sides; but what appealed to me above all was the knowledge that one small boy had insisted on giving the whole of his pocket-money to the presentation from the School. I felt that my labours had not been in vain.

---

14 Ironically Lee Williams outlived Brewer and attended his funeral (see p.179).

– 7 –

Appointment to Gloucester (1896)

When announcing my appointment to Gloucester Cathedral on December 15th, 1896, *The Citizen*, a local newspaper, contained a portrait of myself which had been specially sketched for the paper by George Belcher.[1] The editor, Mr Godwin Chance, in sending me some years later the original line drawing from which the block had been prepared, said:

> I think you might like to have the enclosed. It is the work of one who began a now prosperous career as an artist by doing such work for us before we made use of photography. George Belcher's name is now universally known.

One of the first letters I received after my appointment was from Lloyd, who had ever been to me guide, philosopher and friend. He wrote:

> The good news you tell me was whispered to me yesterday week, but it was in confidence, and I dared not give you even a hint, lest there should be any slip between the cup and the lip. You cannot think what pleasure it gives me to think that after all your disappointments and ill luck you are to get the post for which you have always seemed destined.

In addition to Lloyd's support Sir Walter Parratt, Sir Hubert Parry and Sir John Stainer strongly pressed my claims. Stainer wrote:

---

1   George Frederick Arthur Belcher (1875–1947) was a noted English cartoonist and illustrator. He studied at Gloucester School of Art, and was elected a Royal Academician in 1945. The portrait is facing p.66 in the 1931 edition of Brewer's *Memories*.

South Parks Road
Oxford
Nov. 30, 1896

My dear Brewer
There can be no doubt about the fact that *you* are
the right man for Gloucester, and it has given me great
pleasure to write to the Dean and say so.

Yours truly
J. Stainer

From the time I entered the Cathedral choir as a chorister my
one ambition was to become organist of a cathedral, and this goal
had ever been in my mind. I had been considered at one or two
cathedrals after my short tenure at Bristol, but my wish was not
attained until I was appointed to Gloucester.

My heart has always been in cathedral work and now, after
twenty-eight years as organist, I rejoice to say that my enthusiasm
for the Cathedral services is just as keen as it was when I was a
small chorister. The daily practices with the boys have always been
a source of pleasure, and I think the choristers derive as much
enjoyment from them as I do. Some hundreds of boys have passed
through my hands, and from the first I have made it a rule that every
boy should learn an instrument of some kind. The result, from the
choirmaster's point of view, has been greatly to simplify the work.
All the boys read music fluently, and in consequence I have often
been able to perform a new setting of the canticles or an anthem
with a minimum amount of rehearsal. The knowledge of an instrument is also of untold value to the boys in after-life. Then, again,
I find it a beneficial plan to question the boys as to the singing of
the previous day's service, making them criticize their own performance. It is astonishing how alert and attentive and critical they
become. In the early days here we made use of boys alone for the
services when the lay-clerks were away for their holidays. It was for
this reason, and on account of the ethereal effect produced in the
Cathedral by the boys singing unaccompanied in parts, that I wrote
the responses for treble voices, which seem to have supplied a want
in other cathedrals and elsewhere.[2]

---

2   *Versicles and Responses arranged for Boys' or Ladies' Voices* (Novello & Co. Ltd,
     1901).

I cannot refrain from telling a story against myself in connection with the boys. It happened one afternoon that a Minor Canon reported some of the choristers to me for talking on their fingers during service. He regretted to have to do this, but felt it was his duty. Obeying my instructions the boys were awaiting me in the transept after service, and as I approached them I exclaimed angrily: "What do you mean by talking in the dem and duff alphabet?" This did not sound right so I hastily said, "I mean the duff and dem." Even that felt wrong, and I turned to my assistant with the appeal, "What do I mean?" "Please, sir," he replied, "I think you mean the deaf and dumb alphabet." "Yes, deaf and dumb." By this time the boys had difficulty in concealing their mirth, and my stern talk resolved itself into a feeble dismissal with a warning not to let it happen again!

I have always made a point of not missing a practice or a rehearsal of any kind when it has been at all possible for me to attend. I feel sure this has helped to bring about that *esprit de corps* which exists amongst the members of my choirs and societies. Slackness and lack of enthusiasm on the part of a choirmaster or conductor soon affect those who are placed under his control.

I was not the first Gloucester chorister who eventually found himself occupying the organist's seat. This honour fell to William Mutlow, who was organist of the Cathedral for the long period of fifty years – from 1782 to 1832.[3] He was a man of immense proportions, the lower part of his waistcoat projecting to such an extent that it must have been impossible for him ever to see his feet on the pedals! Report says that when a chorister he fell from the Choir Triforium on to the pavement below and bounced about like an india-rubber ball without coming to any harm, so well covered were his bones! Mutlow is buried in the North Walk of the Cloister, and is the third Gloucester organist who finds a resting-place in that unique fourteenth-century cloister, with its glorious fan-tracery.

The first organist to be buried there was Stephen Jeffries,[4] an eccentric character, judging from the Cathedral records. The record runs as follows:

---

3   See Shaw, *The Succession of Organists*, pp.124–5.
4   For a full account of Stephen Jeffries (d.1713) see Shaw, *op. cit.*, p.122.

A singer from a distant church, with a good voice, had been invited and undertook to sing a solo anthem in the Cathedral, and for that purpose took up his station at the elbow of the organist in the organ-loft. Jeffries, who found him trip in the performance, instead of palliating his mistake and setting him right, immediately rose from his seat and, leaning over the gallery, called out aloud to the choir and the whole congregation, "He can't sing it!"

He was also admonished for playing over upon the organ a common ballad:

insomuch that the young gentlewomen invited one another to dance. And though Dr Gregory (the Senior Prebendary of this Church) did immediately express his great detestation of the same, yet he, the said Stephen Jeffries, in direct despite to religion and affront to the said Dr Gregory, did after Evening Prayer, as soon as the last Amen was ended, in the presence and hearing of all the congregation, fall upon the same strain, and on the organ played over the same common ballad again, insomuch that the young gentlewomen invited one another to dance, and the strangers cried it were better that the organ were pulled down than that they should be so used, and all sorts declared that the Dean and Chapter could never remove the scandal if they did not immediately turn away so insolent and profane a person out of the Church.[5]

To cure him of a habit of staying late at the tavern, his wife dressed up a fellow in a winding-sheet, with directions to meet him with a lanthorn and candle in the cloisters through which he was to pass on his way home; but on attempting to terrify him, Jeffries expressed his wonder only by saying, "I thought all you spirits had been a-bed before this time!"[6] His memory is perpetuated in Gloucester by one of the four tunes played on the Cathedral bells.

---

5   Gloucester Cathedral Chapter Acts (1616–88, for 8 February 1688). See Shaw, *The Succession of Organists*, p.122.
6   Brewer has quoted this anecdote verbatim from the 1853 edition of Hawkins's *A General History of the Science and Practice of Music*, vol.2, p.770.

It is an interesting fact that out of the long line of organists of
Gloucester Cathedral five cover in length of service no less a period
than 181 years, myself being the fifth.[7] This seems to imply that an
organist's lot is not in the same category as Gilbert's Policeman
in *The Pirates of Penzance*.[8] Evidently my predecessors found it a
peaceful and non-nerve-racking occupation. They did little else
beyond the daily routine of the Cathedral services.

Dr Spence-Jones[9] was Dean when I became Organist. He was
not in the least musical and did not pretend to be. He asked me once
whether I was glad or sorry for this. I told him I was glad because,
in consequence, he left all musical matters unquestioningly in my
hands. Unfortunately it cut both ways because, although he did
not interfere with me, there were times when I needed his support
in proposed improvements in connection with the choir, and time
after time my suggested schemes fell through in consequence of
his inability, from lack of musical knowledge, to grasp the benefits
that would result therefrom, and so he failed to give the necessary
support. On one occasion when I was complaining of the flat singing
of a member of the Choir, he turned to me and said: "I have heard
you use that expression, 'flat singing' before, Brewer. What do you
mean by it? Does it mean a note *behind*?"

On taking up my official duties in Gloucester I became Conductor
of the Choral Society. I was not altogether a newcomer to the
Society, as I had officiated as organist and accompanist in my early
days. My first association with it was before I reached my teens as
a nightingale in a Toy-symphony, the golden notes being produced
with a glass tube in a tumbler of water. This Society, which forms the
nursery for the Gloucester contingent of the Three Choirs Festival,
had as its President in those days Joseph Bennett, whose custom it
was to provide the artists for the final concert of the season. This took

---

7   It is clear that Brewer is not referring to himself and his four *immediate*
     predecessors. Brewer's four predecessors with the longest length of service were
     Jeffries (31 years), Smith (42), Mutlow (51) and Amott (33). This suggests that
     Brewer may have written this chapter in about 1920, though the reference (p.51)
     to "twenty-eight years as organist" would suggest a date closer to 1924.
8   "A policeman's lot is not a happy one."
9   The Very Rev'd Henry Donald Maurice Spence-Jones (1836–1917) was an
     authority on the early history of the Christian church. His many publications
     include a four-volume history of the Church of England.

the form of a miscellaneous concert, the chorus only contributing some unaccompanied motets. So widespread was his influence that he was able to obtain the services of the greatest artists of the day. He was in fact so lavish that these veritable feasts of music usually lasted until after eleven o'clock at night, and were then followed by feasts of another kind, with speeches and much merry-making extending into the small hours of the morning.

My first big function in the Cathedral was the celebration of Queen Victoria's Jubilee on June 22nd, 1897, when it was computed that there were between five and six thousand people present. The Cathedral and Voluntary Choirs were augmented by the Gloucester Festival Chorus. An orchestra was engaged, and the music performed included *Zadok the Priest* and Mendelssohn's *Hymn of Praise*. A special feature of the day was the singing of two hymns and the National Anthem at 8 a.m. by a choir of 120 voices on the tower of the Cathedral. Following closely on this memorable anniversary came one of an interesting and unique nature – Mr Alfred Littleton,[10] the Chairman of Novello & Co., invited all the cathedral organists to meet at dinner Sir Frederick Bridge and Sir George Martin, who had recently received the honour of Knighthood from Her Majesty. The cathedral organists with few exceptions accepted the invitation, and there was never such an assembly either before or since. Some capital and highly amusing speeches were made, and one gentleman was so elated at the success of the gathering that he expressed the hope that our host would make it an annual event!

It is now close on fifty years since I began my association with the Three Choirs, the same year in which Lloyd undertook the duties of Conductor.[11] The rehearsals in those days were held in the room in which Wesley died and which is now my drawing-room. It was my duty, when I was not singing, to provide the ladies with iced water when they were on the verge of collapse. The Chorus was drawn from London, Oxford, Cambridge, Wells, Bristol, Leeds, Bradford, Cardiff as well as Gloucester, Worcester and Hereford. We rarely had more than twelve rehearsals at either of the three cities, and the entire chorus never met until the day before the Festival, when the final rehearsal was held.

---

10   1845–1914.
11   i.e. 1877.

Compare this with the preparation for the Gloucester Festival in 1922 when I conducted some eighty rehearsals in addition to four combined rehearsals. The standard of choral performances was naturally not so high as it is now, but on the other hand sight-reading must have been on a much higher level; otherwise such works as Bach's *Passion*[12] and Brahms's *German Requiem*, to mention two only, could never have been learnt in the time.

Daniel Lysons, in his *Origin and Progress of the Meeting of the Three Choirs*, says:[13]

> From the first institution of the Meeting it appears that there were balls for the amusement of the company each night after the concert, but not formerly in the same room. In the Gloucester advertisement, in 1742, is a request that the ballroom might not be opened till the Concert was over. In 1757, the balls, as well as the concerts, were held at the Boothall; which, in the advertisement of that year, is said to have been fitted up for the purpose ...[14]
>
> With a view probably of attracting a still greater influx of company to the Meeting, it was customary for many years to have the Gloucester Races in the Music Meeting week; and as far back as the year 1736, I find four days' sport advertised. In 1754, the races are advertised for Tuesday and Friday, in the Music Meeting week, as they continued many years. On the Tuesday night there was always a ball at the Bell Inn,[15] called the Stewards' ball, at which the Lay-steward of the Meeting, who was also Steward of the races, presided. It was generally attended

---

12   i.e. the *St Matthew Passion*. Bach's *St John Passion* was not heard at a Three Choirs Festival until 1929, the year following Brewer's death. The performance that year (at Worcester) was conducted by Sir Ivor Atkins, whose English-texted edition was published that year by Novello & Co. Ltd.

13   Daniel Lysons (*et al.*), *Origin and Progress of the Meeting of the Three Choirs* ... (Gloucester, 1895), pp.25 & 30. These two paragraphs have been slightly modified so as to restore the 1895 text.

14   The Boothall was located on the south side of Westgate Street, between Berkeley Street and Upper Quay Lane. The hall was demolished in 1957, when the site was subsumed into the extended Shire Hall.

15   Formerly on the east side of Southgate Street very close to 'The Cross', but demolished in the 1960s.

by all the nobility and gentry of the county who were
present at the Meeting. The races and the Stewards' ball
have been discontinued since the year 1793.

The outstanding features of the 1880 Festival were Beethoven's
Mass in D and Scenes from Shelley's *Prometheus Unbound* set
to music by Hubert Parry. This was Parry's first big choral work,
and was specially written for this Meeting. He had appeared at
a Gloucester Festival as far back as 1868, but only with a short
orchestral work – *Intermezzo Religioso* – when he was twenty years
of age. *Prometheus Unbound* caused the chorus much tribulation,
the final rehearsal extending far into the night. This was chiefly due
to the then modern feeling of the work, which troubled the chorus
as much as the incorrectness of the orchestral parts worried the
instrumentalists. The performance suffered in consequence. But
it did not equal the catastrophe which happened at the Hereford
Festival in 1879 when Sullivan conducted his *Light of the World*.
The chorus broke down completely, and a fresh start had to be made.
Sullivan was a stranger to them, and he had only a short rehearsal
before the performance, and as the work was not properly prepared
they were unable to give their undivided attention to his beat.
Considering how few rehearsals were held, it was extraordinary that
more mishaps of this kind did not occur.

How well I remember Sullivan telling me some years later of an
extraordinary experience he had had on the previous evening. It
was the custom of a well-known choir to give a concert consisting
entirely of one composer's works, and the great composer was
invited to conduct. He accepted the invitation and went to direct the
performance, but to his surprise not once did a man or boy look at
his beat during the whole evening! They knew the work well enough,
but it did not occur to them that the composer's interpretation might
be different from their own!

Lloyd came to Gloucester as a young man of twenty-seven, with
practically no experience of cathedral work, but such was his musical
ability and so infectious his enthusiasm that the Festivals took on
a new lease of life. It must be remembered that his colleagues at
Worcester and Hereford were men well over sixty years of age at the
time. It is interesting to compare the programmes of Hereford in
1876 and that of Gloucester in 1877, Lloyd's first Festival:

HEREFORD (1876)	GLOUCESTER (1877)
Elijah	*Elijah*
Messiah	*Messiah*
Creation	*Creation*
Hymn of Praise	*Hymn of Praise*
Samson	*St Paul*
The Last Judgement	*Engedi (Mount of Olives)*
St Cecilia (Gounod)	*German Requiem* (Brahms)
The Raising of Lazarus (Barnett)	*The St Matthew Passion* (Bach)

The *German Requiem* had never previously been heard at a Three Choirs Festival, and *The Passion*[16] only once, when it was performed at Gloucester in 1871, conducted by Wesley.

The contrast in the secular concerts was even more marked, that at Hereford consisting of such items as – *Nazareth*, Gounod; *The Pilgrim of Love*, Bishop; *The Wolf*, Shield; *Tom Bowling*, Dibdin; *Now Tramp*, Bishop; etc; whilst at Gloucester were performed Schumann's *Paradise and the Peri* and Gade's *Crusaders*, in addition to Beethoven's Symphony in C minor, Mendelssohn's Violin Concerto, and new orchestral works by Montague Smith[17] and C. V. Stanford.[18] This was Stanford's first appearance at a Three Choirs Festival.

To Gloucester fell the honour of introducing *Messiah* at a Three Choirs Festival. It happened in the year 1757, and was performed in the Boothall. It was received with rapturous applause, and has been repeated at every succeeding Meeting of the Three Choirs, excepting Worcester in 1775. To use Dr Burney's expression, "it has fed the hungry, clothed the naked, fostered the orphan, and enriched the managers of oratorios, more than any single musical performance in this or any country."[19] Gloucester was privileged too to be the first to perform Handel's *Judas Maccabæus* in 1754 and Bach's *St Matthew Passion*, in 1871.

16 Unspecific references to 'The Passion' at this period are invariably to the *St Matthew Passion*, an English-texted edition of which (by Elgar and Atkins) was published by Novello & Co. Ltd in 1911.
17 George Montague Smith (1843–1923), who spent most of his working life in Scotland, had written a *Concert Overture* for the 1877 Gloucester Festival.
18 Stanford's composition was his *Festival Overture* (currently unpublished).
19 Charles Burney (1726–1814) published his four-volume *History of Music* between 1776 and 1789.

The historian continues:[20]

A novel and very interesting feature in the arrangements of this Meeting was the holding of full Cathedral Service each morning (Tuesday excepted) in the choir at eight o'clock. All the members of the Three Choirs assisted at these services, and the attendance of the public was numerous, the admittance being free ...

The institution of early morning services at these Meetings has given much satisfaction, and has removed the scruples of many persons who were hostile to the musical performances in the Cathedral on the ground that they interfered with the legitimate object of the sacred edifice – that of divine worship.

Suggestions had been made from time to time by the clerical Stewards to give a religious character to these Meetings, one of which was to commence each morning's performance with a portion of the Church Service; but this, on reflection, was obviously impracticable. The proposal of the early services, so happily carried out, was the suggestion of Mr Amott, the organist of the Cathedral.

The music performed at these services comprised –

Tallis's Responses and Litany
Rogers's Service in D
Gibbons's Service in F
Croft's Service in A

And the anthems –

Cry aloud and shout	Croft
Hosanna to the Son of David	Gibbons
Lord, for Thy tender mercy's sake	(ascribed to) Farrant

The example set at Gloucester, in 1853, of holding full Cathedral Service each morning, was followed at Worcester ...

It is a curious and amusing fact that for many years prior to 1880 the Festival ticket office was managed by a Mr 'Nest', who was eventually succeeded in the business by Mr 'Partridge'. He had as his partner a Mr 'Robins', and the ticket office was then for some years

---

20 Lysons (*op. cit.*), pp.174 & 177. This passage has been slightly modified so as to restore the 1895 text.

in the charge of Messrs. 'Partridge' and 'Robins'. Their names hardly suggest any connection with singing birds!

Speaking of birds brings back to my memory an amusing episode at the Hereford Festival of 1897. The opening service took place on the Sunday morning. It was a warm sultry day, and the Dean and Chapter thought it necessary to ventilate the Cathedral as much as possible before the service began. All the doors and windows were accordingly opened at an early hour. The coolness of the building attracted a little robin inside. It remained perfectly quiet, perched high up in the lantern tower, till Sinclair began to conduct the *Unfinished Symphony*. Then it opened out its little heart, and had a good deal to say to the Band and Chorus for disturbing its peace. The antics of the bird were so distracting that it was difficult to give undivided attention to the performance of Schubert's beautiful work, or, in fact, to the remainder of the service. At the close every effort was made to entice the bird out of the building, but in vain. Sinclair felt that he could not continue to conduct the Festival with the robin's opposition, so a bird-catcher's services were enlisted. He brought in a decoy-bird and a twig covered with bird-lime. This proved effective, for the robin was soon caught, and his song became another unfinished symphony so far as the Hereford Festival was concerned.

A rather pretty bird experience fell to my lot one summer evening when I was sitting smoking in the garden in front of my house. I heard a rustling in the bush behind me; presently a young blackbird flew out and sat on the garden seat beside me. I remained perfectly still, watching it. It evidently felt secure from harm, for after a time it perched on my knee and looked up into my face as if to say, "At last I have found a friend." It remained on my knee for some few moments whilst the parent birds, in great agitation, flew round and round the garden using most awful bird language, no doubt telling their offspring what they thought of me. But my newly found friend remained undismayed and quite content until it caught sight of its parents carrying a tempting morsel on to the doorstep of my house. That proved too enticing and it deserted me.

But I digress.

It was for the Hereford Festival in 1897 that I prepared my first chorus contingent for a Three Choirs Festival. Speaking in high terms of the chorus, a leading critic said:

It was plainly evident that the three cities are wholly independent of the "small contingent from Leeds" announced in the programme. The choir may be trusted with anything, and the additional incentive of confidence would carry them through any work now known. Mr Brewer of Gloucester has a great opportunity, and we wait with some interest the result of this suggestion. Courage only is needed. Let Gloucester have the glory of being the first to do without extraneous help.

I did not need this suggestion, for I had already determined that the chorus for my first Festival, in 1898, should be drawn entirely from the three counties of Gloucester, Worcester and Hereford. This was accomplished with the happiest results, the Press speaking in the highest terms of praise of the work done by the chorus. One critic, in summing up the Festival, says:

We must give unstinted praise to the Chorus, whose work was marked by enthusiasm from beginning to end. Let the magnates of Worcester foster the esprit de corps which, in such matters, is inestimable, by respectfully doing without the "small contingent from Leeds." If Gloucester can rely on itself, why not Worcester?

But more of the '98 Festival anon. Owing to the Hereford Festival falling in Queen Victoria's Jubilee Year, special music was chosen for the occasion. The performance of *Elijah*, which usually opens the proceedings, was postponed to a later day; *Zadok the Priest* and a *Hymn of Thanksgiving* for the Queen's long reign, specially written by Lloyd, and the *Hymn of Praise* were performed in its place. The chief choral work was Beethoven's *Mass in D*. In view of the trying nature of the choral music, the 'normal' or low pitch, was adopted for this performance only. It was to be wished that the whole of the Festival music could have been sung at the same diapason normal, but this would have involved a very heavy addition to the week's work; for the *Mass* alone it was necessary for me to transpose the whole of the organ part a semitone lower, a sufficiently arduous task. A special feature at the opening service was a new setting of the *Te Deum* and *Benedictus* by Elgar.

As is usual at Hereford the Festival ended with a chamber concert, at which a partsong of mine found a place. This was not my first appearance as a composer at a Three Choirs Festival, for works of a similar character had been performed at Gloucester in 1892 and at Hereford in 1894.[21]

It was at one of the Three Choirs Festivals that a Steward gently informed a lady that she was occupying the wrong seat. With indignation she replied: "I sat in this seat for *The Creation* and I intend to remain here for *The Last Judgement!*"

---

21 According to Lysons (*op. cit.*), pp.304 & 311, at the 1892 Gloucester Festival Brewer conducted his 'pretty' partsong *Song and Summer*, and at the 1894 Hereford Festival the Leeds contingent of the festival chorus performed his partsong *Sad Hearts* 'in a finished style'.

– 8 –

The Gloucester Three Choirs Festival (1898)

I cannot pass over this period of my career without alluding to Mrs Ellicott,[1] the wife of the Bishop of Gloucester. She was devoted to music, especially to the music of Handel and Spohr, and she was one of the founders of the Handel Society in London – a choral body inaugurated to perform the works of the old Master. Her daughter, Miss Rosalind Ellicott, wrote more than one work for the Three Choirs Festival at Gloucester, and was a soprano vocalist of no mean ability.[2] Her services were much in request at charitable concerts in the county.

Mrs Ellicott possessed a rich contralto voice, and both mother and daughter were excellent readers. They were never happier than when they had their intimate friends around them at the Palace singing unaccompanied music. Their musical library was an extensive one, and they were able, on these occasions, to sing much madrigalian music of the Elizabethan period in addition to that of modern writers. It was the custom for these music-makings to take place immediately after tea, and they were often continued after dinner. The singers, numbering from eight to twelve, would sit round an oval table with their music before them and at their side a tumbler of egg-flip! A most soothing lubrication for the vocal chords which all appreciated.

Mrs Ellicott was the founder of the Gloucestershire Philharmonic Society – a Society which she started as soon as Lloyd came to Gloucester, and which consisted mainly of members living outside the city. For their convenience the rehearsals and concerts took

---

1   Constantia Annie Ellicott (1828–1914) was the daughter of Admiral Alexander Becher (1796–1876).
2   Rosalind Ellicott (1857–1924) was a very capable pianist also. Her compositions *The Birth of Song*, the *Fantasie in A minor for Piano and Orchestra*, and *Henry of Navarre* were performed at the Gloucester Festivals of 1892, 1895 and 1898 respectively.

place in the afternoon.[3] It was at one of these concerts, when Sir Julius Benedict came to conduct his oratorio *St Cecilia*, which was produced at the Norwich Festival of 1866, that Lloyd presided at the organ. The organ had an important part to play in the work, and in one place was the solo instrument. But when the time came for the solo there was no wind in the organ – this was before the days of electric blowers – and no sound was heard. Lloyd immediately shouted down the speaking tube: "Blow, you fools, or I'll come down and punch your heads!" The audience, delighted with this little interlude, received it with shouts of laughter. It must be remembered that Lloyd was a young man at the time, and had not lost the exuberance of youth.

Mrs Ellicott's 'At Homes', whether in London or Gloucester, were always the rendezvous of social celebrities. At her residence in Great Cumberland Place one met such actors as Henry Irving,[4] Wilson Barrett,[5] Forbes-Robertson[6] and J. L. Toole,[7] and from the musical world Piatti,[8] Goring Thomas[9] and many others. I remember meeting Goring Thomas at dinner there before the production of his opera *Nadeshda*.[10] He was a most genial and entertaining person, and the world of music became the poorer by his early death.

These musical 'At Homes' were often wearisome to the Bishop,[11] who disliked music as much as his wife and daughter loved it. Arriving home one winter afternoon he found his wife and daughter entertaining some friends. They were singing a duet. The fire was black and cheerless; the Bishop took up the poker and began to stir it vigorously. Mrs Ellicott stopped singing and, in a reproachful voice exclaimed, "My dear, my dear!" The Bishop, holding up his hand in

---

3   For further information on the contribution of Constantia Ellicott to the musical life of Gloucester, see Boden, pp.70–71.
4   Sir Henry Irving (1838–1905) was the first actor to be knighted.
5   Wilson Barrett (1846–1904).
6   Sir Johnston Forbes-Robertson (1853–1937).
7   John Lawrence Toole (1830–1906).
8   Alfredo Piatti (1822–1901), Italian 'cellist.
9   Arthur Goring Thomas (1850–92), composer.
10 *Nadeshda* (1885), the fourth and finest of Goring Thomas's five operas, was commissioned by the Carl Rosa Opera Company.
11 The Rt Rev'd Charles John Ellicott (1819–1905). He relinquished the combined Bishoprics of Bristol and Gloucester in 1897, within months of Brewer's appointment at Gloucester.

a becalming manner, replied, "Don't stop, my love, don't stop! You don't disturb me in the least!"

I remember one Sunday afternoon after Wesley's *Wilderness* had been sung in the Cathedral, he said to me: "Brewer, I don't like that anthem you gave us this afternoon." "Don't you, my Lord? It is supposed to be one of Wesley's finest." "Oh, I am not complaining about the music. I'm complaining about the length. I don't know where Dr Wesley has gone; but all I can say is, that if he still composes anthems that length, they won't keep him in either place very long!" Long anthems bored him. He often told me that he spent the time, during their performance, translating the words into Hebrew and Greek, and, if they were particularly long, into Arabic as well.

The Bishop had the misfortune to have both his legs broken in a railway accident. When he was discovered after this terrible disaster occurred, he was tending the dying, and urged the rescuers to look after those who were more seriously hurt than himself. It was probably due to this that he never wore gaiters. A newly appointed Archdeacon, unaware of the accident, asked him why he never wore gaiters. The Bishop, in his thin, piping voice, replied: "Well, you see, if I wore gaiters, I might be taken for an Archdeacon!" In his young days he spent most of his holidays mountaineering and skating; he was an expert in both sports.

The Gloucester Festival has always had an advantage over those held at the sister cities in being able to make use of the Cathedral organ during the performances. The orchestra is built up in the centre of the Cathedral against the screen, the organ forming a background; whilst at Worcester and Hereford the orchestra is placed at the west end, which necessitates the erection of a temporary organ for the week, a makeshift instrument, sometimes, as at Hereford in 1921, without pedals. Not only is Gloucester favoured by being able to use its own organ, but it is generally recognized as being a perfect building for sound. All the great singers who have sung at the Festivals agree on this point.

Pride in their own cathedral is a characteristic of the singers attached to each place. I recollect, when wandering round one of the sister cathedrals before a Festival performance, meeting a local enthusiast to whom I expressed the opinion that their cathedral was beautiful, but it did not equal Gloucester either in architecture or acoustics. "Our cathedral," he indignantly retorted, "is easy enough to sing in for those who know *how* to sing," and added, "*I* have never had any difficulty."!

Soon after my arrival in Gloucester, I raised the question of completing the organ by adding the solo organ and the pedal stops which had been contemplated, but never carried out in the restoration in 1888. An appeal was issued under the signatures of Dean Spence and myself, and within a few months the sum of £654 (Willis's estimate) was collected by subscription and by giving organ recitals for the fund. Henry Willis refused to contemplate the introduction of an electric blower, regarding it as 'dangerous and unreliable', and suggested a hydraulic engine as the best practical method of superseding "the arms of three strong men for ordinary services." I was anxious to have the organ completed for my first Festival, and when my friend, Mr R. G. Foster,[12] a real benefactor in musical as well as other matters in the city, heard of this he came forward, and, in addition to giving a substantial donation, generously undertook to be responsible for the money until the amount had been collected. Unfortunately the work was not quite finished in time for the Festival that year (1898). The organ was not actually completed until the following January, when it was formally opened.

It was for the closing service – which proved to be the last one of its kind – of the Festival in 1895 that I wrote an orchestral setting of the canticles in C,[13] which has been repeated at several opening services since. It was whilst staying at Newquay that I scored this setting of the canticles. My landlady seemed to be interested in what I was doing, so I told her that I was writing a work to be performed at the Gloucester Festival, and added, I suppose you have heard of the Gloucester Festival". "Oh no, sir," she replied, "we are church people, we are!" I never discovered to what sect she thought I belonged.

After the Festival of 1895 a special committee was appointed to consider and report to the standing committee as to the best mode of assuring the financial success of future festivals. In their report they drew attention to the fees paid to the principal singers,

---

12   Foster, a prominent Gloucester Magistrate and businessman, was Chairman of the Gloucester Harbour Board. Together with Godwin Chance (see below, p.78) he was a member of the local tribunal which scrutinised applications for exemption from military service during the 1914–18 war.

13   This setting, for solo soprano, chorus and orchestra, was published by Novello, Ewer & Co. (1895).

which, they said, were increasing year by year, and a stand would have to be made. They also found that the Friday evening Cathedral service was undoubtedly prejudicial to the funds of the Charity, and recommended that the Festival should close with *Messiah.* "Many people," they went on to say, "satisfy their musical requirements and their charitable consciences by going only to this free service." It is interesting to record the conclusion at which they arrived with regard to novelties. They said:

> We would emphatically point out that the number of new works presented at the Gloucester Festivals is very much larger than is the case elsewhere. It is unfortunately a fact that they are often produced at a loss, and as this loss falls heavily on the Charity, we are of opinion that only one new work should be given at the next Festival, and its production should entail no extra expense upon the Festival funds.

It might be mentioned that the fees paid to the four principal singers for the 1895 Festival nearly doubled those of all the artists for the 1898 Meeting. Only one of the principal performers of 1895 appeared at the next Festival, and who will say that the work was not as well done! The days when audiences were attracted chiefly by star-artists were fast disappearing.

The suggestion of abolishing the closing service on the Friday evening was wise and sensible, but the committee, in their report, had not suggested anything to take its place. I therefore proposed, when arrangements were being made for the Festival of 1898, that there should be an opening service with full chorus and orchestra on the Sunday preceding the Festival, and pointed out the advantages of such an arrangement. In the first place there was the very practical gain of having the chorus and orchestra for an additional rehearsal on the Saturday. The effect, too, of a great opening musical service would be to whet the appetites of those present, so that after hearing such a performance they would be like Oliver Twist and want more. It would also enable the members of the orchestra and chorus to settle down and get accustomed to their surroundings before the Festival proper began.

The question of new works was a different matter altogether. I pointed out that if musical interest was not maintained, and if the programmes contained no novelties, the Festivals would soon cease to attract, and would pass away like other worn-out institutions. Taste and education in music were developing with such rapid strides that Festival Committees had to realize that the chief attraction was the music itself. This counsel fortunately now prevails, and it is recognized that the art of music does not stand still, and that, in drawing up a programme, the artistic side must be considered as well as the Charity. The Stewards thereupon decided to invite Sir Hubert Parry, Sir John Stainer, Dr Lloyd, Mr Lee Williams and myself to write new works. Stainer was unable to accept the invitation. Lloyd's contribution was a Festival Overture; Lee Williams wrote a setting of the canticles;[14] and my work was *The 98th Psalm*;[15] all of which were performed at the opening service of the Festival.

It is interesting to record that it was on this occasion that Sir Edward Elgar's name appeared for the first time in a Gloucester Festival programme. The work chosen was 'The Meditation' from *Lux Christi*, which was performed at the opening service.[16] The composer conducted. Sir Hubert Parry wrote *A Song of Darkness and Light*, and Dr Harwood's new work *Inclina Domine* was performed; and it was our privilege to give the first performance in England of three new works by Verdi: (1) *Stabat Mater*; (2) *Laudi alla Vergine Maria*; (3) *Te Deum*.[17] Had the committee persisted in the exclusion of novelties the honour of producing these works at a Three Choirs Festival would not have been ours.

Lastly, but by no means least, I persuaded the Stewards to invite Coleridge-Taylor to write a new orchestral work for the secular concert in the Shire Hall. This composer's name was unknown at the time, and his colour, as well as his music, caused a sensation. How his name was brought forward is worthy of record; Elgar was

---

14   This was his Service in C, No.2 (Novello & Co. Ltd, 1898).
15   *O sing unto the Lord a new song*, for soprano and bass soloists, choir and orchestra (Novello & Co., 1898).
16   Op.29. Although at first known as *Lux Christi* Elgar was persuaded by his publisher (Novello) to give this oratorio an English title, for which he chose *The Light of Life*. It had received its first performance at the Worcester Festival of 1896 under the composer's direction.
17   Together with Verdi's *Ave Maria* (1889) these later became known as his *Quattro Pezzi Sacri*. The works were composed independently and brought together as a set only in 1898.

at this time, by his great genius, forging his way to the front, and the Stewards, acting on my suggestion, invited him to write an orchestral work for the Festival. I received the following letter from him in reply:

> Forii
> Malvern
> April 17, 1898

> Dear Mr Brewer
>   I have received a request from the Secretary to write a short orchestral thing for the Evening Concert. I am sorry I am too busy to do so.
>   I *wish, wish, wish* you would ask Coleridge-Taylor to do it. He still wants recognition and is far away the cleverest fellow going amongst the young men. *Please* don't let your Committee throw away the chance of doing a good act!

> Yours sincerely
> Edward Elgar

A month later I received a letter from A. J. Jaeger,[18] who was then head of the Publishing Department at Novello & Co. His death, in 1909, caused a blank in the musical world which has never been filled. He was so honest and helpful in his criticisms that his advice was sought by all who had the good fortune to know him. He was a true friend to Coleridge-Taylor from every point of view, a fact to which the following letter bears testimony:

> London
> May 12, 1898

> Dear Mr Brewer
>   My friend Mr Elgar told me a week ago that he had refused an offer to write an orchestral work for your

---

18 Jaeger's memory is perpetuated in 'Nimrod', Variation 9 of Elgar's *Variations on an Original Theme* (Op.36). The copious correspondence between Elgar and Jaeger is documented in Jerrold Northrop Moore (ed.), *Elgar and his Publishers*, 2 vols (Oxford, 1987).

Festival, I am glad to hear it for *his* sake for he has his hands full with "Caractacus" and the haste with which most of you good men have to compose their Festival works is on the whole the great bane of English music. Everybody seems to write under fearful pressure (especially Parry) and the consequences we all know, alas! Well, it is not my business, but I am awfully sorry it is so.

My object in writing is to draw your attention to a young friend of mine, S. Coleridge-Taylor, who is most wonderfully gifted and might write your committee a *fine* work in a short time. He has a quite Schubertian facility of invention and his stuff is always original and fresh. He is the coming man, I'm quite sure! He is only 22 or 23 but there is nothing immature or inartistic about his music. It is worth a great deal to me – I mean I value it very highly, because it is so original and often *beautiful*. Here is a real melodist at last.

Why not try him and make the '98 Festival memorable by the introduction of young S. C-T. He scores very well, in fact he conceives everything orchestrally and never touches the P.F.[19] when composing! I suppose you know that his father is a negro. Hence his wonderful *freshness*.

Why not give him a commission? He would rise to the occasion and do something good.

His symphony in A minor is a most original work. We are doing a short Cantata of his, "Hiawatha's Wedding Feast"; delightful stuff! Won't *that* do for your Festival? You want a secular work don't you? I'll send you the MS score (P.F.) if you like (though at present in the printer's hands). At any rate you keep your eye on the lad, and believe me, he is *the* man of the future in musical England.

Yours faithfully
A. J. Jaeger

An invitation was accordingly extended to Coleridge-Taylor to write an orchestral work. His *Ballade in A minor* was the outcome, and the sensation caused by the work on account of all the points which Mr Jaeger emphasizes in his letter to me is now a matter

---

19   i.e. *pianoforte*.

of history. It therefore transpired that, in spite of the committee's resolution to exclude new works from the programme, no less than nine appeared in the scheme. The inclusion of the *Ballade* and the new works by Verdi, and the dispensing with extraneous help in the chorus were among the chief features which helped to make the '98 Festival a memorable one. The Italian papers were enthusiastic in their report of the performance of the great master's works; and, to show his appreciation, Verdi not only sent a letter full of gratitude, but the following Christmas I received from him a signed photograph which I greatly value, more especially as it was not his wont to bestow such gifts.[20]

In summing up the week's music *The Daily Telegraph* says:

> It is interesting to note how many musicians engaged at this Festival belong by birth to Gloucestershire. Among the composers are Dr Lloyd, Mr Brewer and Mr Basil Harwood; among the vocalists, Miss Nicholls[21] and Mr Watkin Mills;[22] while others intimately connected with the county, if not born within its limits, include Sir Hubert Parry, Miss Hilda Wilson, and Mr H. Lane Wilson.[23]
>
> Gloucestershire certainly has a right to be festive in music.

The attendance exceeded that of the previous Festival by 200, the figures being 14,367 as against 14,145. Taking the aggregate and noting how it was made up, I find *Messiah* in its old place of supremacy. The oratorio attracted 3,286, as against 3,142 by *Elijah*. How significant, as regards the position of these two works, is the fact that, out of the grand total of 14,367 attendances, 6,428, or only 755 less than half, were due to their power of attraction.

The complete programme was as follows:

---

20 It is regrettable that Brewer chose not to quote Verdi's letter of appreciation. It is not known whether the letter still exists.

21 Agnes Nicholls (1876–1959), a versatile soprano, was born in Cheltenham. She performed privately before Queen Victoria on three occasions.

22 Robert Watkin Mills (1849–1930), a bass-baritone, was born in Painswick and studied with Samuel Sebastian Wesley. He appeared at several Promenade Concerts before emigrating to Canada in 1914.

23 Matilda Ellen Wilson (1860–1907), known as 'Hilda', was a Gloucester-born contralto, whose father was a bandmaster and publican. The composer and singer Henry Lane Wilson (1871–1915) was her brother. See Boden, p.85.

Sunday September 11

Festival Overture	C. H. Lloyd
Magnificat and Nunc dimittis	C. Lee Williams
98th Psalm	A. Herbert Brewer
Meditation (Lux Christi)	Edward Elgar

Tuesday Morning

Elijah	Mendelssohn

Tuesday Evening

Stabat Mater	Dvořák
The Creation	Haydn

Wednesday Morning

Organ Concerto in E minor	Prout
In Exitu Israel	Wesley[24]
Three New Works	Verdi
Variations 'St. Antoni'	Brahms
Hymn of Praise	Mendelssohn

Wednesday Evening

Meistersinger Overture	Wagner
Henry of Navarre	R. Ellicott
Ballade in A minor	Coleridge-Taylor
The Golden Legend[25]	Sullivan

Thursday Morning

A Song of Darkness and Light	Parry
Symphony (No.3) in E flat	Beethoven
Adagio and Finale (from Symphony No.5)[26]	Stanford
Christmas Oratorio (Parts 1 and 2)	Bach

---

24   i.e. Samuel Wesley (1766–1837), not Samuel Sebastian.
25   This transpired to be the last performance of *The Golden Legend* at a Three Choirs Festival. See Boden, p.98.
26   This is presumably a reference to the third and fourth movements, although Stanford's own description of the third movement is 'Andante molto tranquillo' rather than 'Adagio'.

Thursday Evening

Inclina Domine	Harwood
Symphony in G minor[27]	Mozart
Judas Maccabæus	Handel

Friday Morning

Messiah	Handel

---

27   No.40 (K.550).

– 9 –

Festival Stewardship; Other conducting experiences

The question of Stewardship at the Three Choirs Festivals has often proved a very serious one for those who have undertaken the duties. Their lot has not always run on smooth and pleasant lines. From 1724 to 1799 there were only two Stewards, and they engaged and defrayed the expenses of the band, and were responsible for losses. At times this came to a considerable amount. For instance, at Gloucester in 1769 the Bishop and his coadjutor were £100 a-piece out of pocket.

> At Hereford, in 1786, ... the gentlemen who had been nominated as Stewards, fearful that the undertaking would be attended at more than usual loss, declined the office, and much difficulty occurred in procuring others to undertake it ...[1]

From 1800 onwards the number of Stewards was increased, and the responsibilities of those who undertook the position were thereby lessened. The historian mentions that in 1832:

> The cholera still lingering in Gloucester, it was decided to charge a small sum for admission to the Cathedral on the first morning, to prevent the assembling together of a crowd of people, which had hitherto been the case, to the great discomfort of the visitors.[2]

There was a large deficiency of £1,365 divisible between six Stewards. In spite of this heavy loss on the music side a considerable sum, no less than £811, was collected for the Charity. In 1838 the

---

1   This quotation, cited by Brewer without a source reference, is from Daniel Lysons, *Origin and Progress of the Meeting of the Three Choirs* ... (Gloucester, 1895), pp.65–6. Brewer's account has been slightly modified here so as to restore Lysons's original text.
2   Lysons (*op. cit.*), p.121.

Gloucester Meeting (or 'Festival', as it was then designated in the programme) was held under the especial patronage of Her Most Gracious Majesty the Queen, and since then the Festivals have always been under Royal Patronage.[3]

The number of Stewards grew from two in the year 1724 to no less than 204 in 1898, my first Festival. Prior to this year the question of inviting ladies to become Stewards had been discussed on more than one occasion. The question was revived again in 1898, Dr Batten championing their cause as he previously had done. Many Stewards were afraid of the "new woman", and wanted to know whether it would mean the flitting of ladies about the Cathedral, or would they be content to attend the Meeting of Stewards only. On a show of hands being taken, a large majority voted against the proposition.

It was revived again before the Festival of 1901. After considerable discussion the question was put to the vote, and it was again decided by a large majority in the negative. Once again in 1904 Dr Batten said he could not believe that there was amongst the 207 Stewards the same want of gallantry as there was three years before when the proposal was defeated. He pointed out that they had Queen Alexandra as a Patroness of the Festival, and they knew that the Princess of Wales[4] and ladies of title were taking various positions in public life. Ladies, both as soloists and members of the chorus, played a prominent part in contributing to the success of the Festivals, and it did seem to him a want of gallantry on the part of the Stewards to prevent the funds being increased by the recognition as Stewards of ladies of position and independent means who were the heads of their own establishment in the county.

One Steward said that he presumed the proposer did not mean that the head of the establishment and his wife would be eligible, otherwise they might have a Steward and a Stewardess. It was pointed out that 'Stewardess' was such a dangerous title, associated as it was with journeys by sea, and recalling unpleasant maritime memories, that the proposer was afraid to use it! Again the proposal

---

3   HRH The Prince of Wales has been President of the Three Choirs Festival Association since 2001.

4   Princess Mary of Teck, who became Queen Consort in 1910 on the Accession of King George V.

was negatived. The project was eventually carried when preparations were being made for the 1907 Festival, and ladies were invited to become Stewards. At the final meeting of Stewards at the close of the Festival one member remarked that he thought the Festival would be remembered as one in connection with which a controversy had been settled which was almost as old as the deceased wife's sister question[5] – that in regard to inviting ladies to become Stewards. They had at length decided that question in the affirmative, and he was almost sorry they had done so, because it would prevent the Stewards having these discussions on the subject, to which they had been accustomed, and which called forth a good deal of eloquence. However, they had settled the question, but, unfortunately the ladies did not seem to wish to take advantage of the opportunity of becoming Stewards, for out of 150 who had been invited, not one accepted the invitation. They *all* declined!

Joseph Bennett, in *The Daily Telegraph* of December 15, 1906, commenting on the arrangements for the Festival of 1907 says:

> For several Festivals past Dr Batten has been the champion of those among the aggressive sex who wish to share with men the honours of stewardship. I noticed at Hereford last September that a small, but doubtless choice representation of abounding feminity had adorned fair bosoms with the official rosette ... If Dr Batten imagines that in the present temper of the sex, the ladies are coming in on any terms save those of perfect equality with men, he most probably is under a delusion. They will certainly decline exclusion from the executive committee, and if they get there – we shall see what we shall see. It may be, however, that the Gloucestershire ladies are not up-to-date. In that lamentable case their condition will, no doubt, call forth the pity and excite the missionary zeal of Misses Kennedy and Pankhurst.[6]

---

5   This is a reference to the then highly topical Deceased Wife's Sister Marriage Act, which removed the prohibition on a man marrying the sister of his deceased wife. The Act was passed in 1907, the year in which ladies eventually became eligible to be Festival Stewards.
6   Annie Kennedy and Christabel Pankhurst were the first suffragettes to be imprisoned.

Much has happened since the days of these discussions. Happily the 'Gloucestershire ladies' are now quite prepared to undertake the responsibilities of stewardship without wishing to 'flit about the Cathedral', for in 1922 no less than one hundred and thirty-seven became Stewards,[7] and at the final meeting after the Festival a vote of thanks "to the Dean and Chapter for the use of the Cathedral and to the Dean for kindly preaching the sermon" was moved by the youngest lady Steward present – Miss Carew Sinnott,[8] aged 15!

The Gloucester and Bristol Diocesan Choral Union (Bristol has since been separated from the See of Gloucester) was one of the organizations I conducted when I first came to the city. The Festival Service generally took place in the Cathedral in June of each year, and many of the choirs in the Diocese journeyed to the Mother Church in all kinds of conveyances, from the squire's carriage and pair to the wagon drawn by a team of horses. It was an impressive sight both inside and outside the building at these annual gatherings. To many of the songsters it was the most important event of the year. A choirmaster was sent from Gloucester to the neighbouring villages to superintend the preparation for the great day. At one small village, on his first visit, he wished to know how the voices were distributed. He began making inquiries as to which part was sung by each adult member of the choir. The first man replied that he generally took the (h)air. Whether that implied that he spent his time in snaring game, or poaching on the trebles' preserves, I cannot say! The second man informed the choir trainer that he sang bass, but it was soon discovered that he really sang the treble part two octaves below! A third said that he sang seconds, which, as a matter of fact, was an attempt to sing a third below the tune. It will be seen from this what difficulties had to be faced before the singers assembled in the Cathedral. These village songsters resemble the orchestral player who expressed a wish to join my Orchestral Society, and on being asked what he played, promptly replied that his instrument was a second violin!

At my first Diocesan Choral Festival nearly forty choirs took part, the number of voices totalling about 1,000. In addition to the

---

7   In 1925 the number was increased to 237.
8   Carew Sinnott (1908–2008) was one of seven children of Colonel Edward Sinnott (County Surveyor for Gloucestershire from 1907 to 1935). See below, p.104.

organ we had drums and brass instruments, which greatly added to the effect and considerably helped the singers. The music performed was of the simplest kind, and of a broad, diatonic character. The result was often very beautiful and inspiring. After a time it was felt that these gatherings had fulfilled their object, which was to raise the standard of singing and the choice of music in the village churches. There were more opportunities for villagers to hear good music than hitherto, largely due to the advent of the motor, which brought these outlying districts into closer touch with the towns; small Choral Societies sprang up – there are quite a large number in this county – and last but not least the village organist of the present day is much better qualified than his predecessor.

In November, 1898, a movement was set on foot to form a male-voice choir in Gloucester. The idea was inspired by the enormous success attending the experiment at the Gloucester Festival of confining the chorus to the three counties. A large body of male-voice singers had been drawn from the city and county for that purpose, and these men were invited to become members of a proposed 'Orpheus Society'. The project was taken up with enthusiasm, and weekly rehearsals were at once started. I acted as Conductor until the Great War, when it was felt that such a Society should suspend its work for the time being.[9] Subsequently I was compelled to resign the conductorship owing to my increased activities in other directions.

During the sixteen years I acted as Conductor many works were specially written for the Society, Parry, Lloyd, Lee Williams, Hathaway[10] and West[11] being among the composers who contributed to their programmes. I was invited by the Hereford Festival Committee to take the 'Orphans' – as the Society, through a printer's error, has more than once been called – to sing at their Festival in 1900, and also to write a work for the occasion. The outcome of this invitation was *Love's Philosophy*, the words of which were written by my friend, Mr Godwin Chance,[12] whose ready pen has

---

9 The Gloucester Orpheus Society, of which Parry was at one time the President, was re-established after the First World War. It ceased to exist in about 1960.

10 Joseph W. G. Hathaway (1870–1956).

11 John E. West (1863–1929).

12 H. Godwin Chance was Editor of the Gloucester daily evening newspaper, *The Citizen* (see above, p.50). He collaborated with Charles Lee Williams in updating Lysons's *Origin and Progress of the Meeting of the Three Choirs* ... (Gloucester, 1895).

been the means of supplying words for other works in which we have collaborated since those days.[13] On two occasions the Society combined with the Royal Bristol Orpheus Society, and gave two concerts on consecutive nights in Gloucester and Bristol in aid of local charities. The effect of the combined West of England forces will not be forgotten by those who were privileged to hear these 170 male voices.

A popular custom in Gloucester, which had been inaugurated by my predecessor C. Lee Williams in 1886, was the giving of fortnightly free recitals in the nave of the Cathedral during the winter months. They consisted of organ solos, vocal and instrumental numbers and a choral item or two. They were originally intended for the very poor, who could not afford the pleasure of a concert, and were financed by a few philanthropic citizens. As time wore on they came to be patronized by well-to-do people, and it was considered only right that the people who enjoyed the music should pay the piper, and, accordingly, a collection was made at the doors to defray the expenses. In recent years they have been reduced in number, and are given chiefly on Bank Holiday afternoons in order to make it possible for the inhabitants of the surrounding country to attend. The choral items are now omitted. The townspeople also have an opportunity of hearing a short organ recital every Sunday afternoon throughout the year.

A very attractive event held every September – with the exception of the year in which the Gloucester Festival took place – was the one-day Festival at Tewkesbury. Well-known artists were engaged – it was at Tewkesbury, I think, that Miss Muriel Foster[14] made her first appearance as a Festival singer – and the chorus was drawn from the Festival contingents of Gloucester and Worcester, and also Tewkesbury. I conducted, and in 1899 wrote a new work for the Festival, Madame Ella Russell being the soloist.[15] Tewkesbury is just

---

13 Godwin Chance supplied the words for Brewer's patriotic marching song *Brothers in Arms*, and for his male voice partsong *The Toast*, which was published in the *Orpheus* series in 1899.

14 The contralto Muriel Foster (1877–1937), a friend of Elgar, was particularly noted for her interpretation of the part of The Angel in Elgar's *The Dream of Gerontius*.

15 American-born soprano (1864–1935). The new work may have been *As the earth bringeth forth her bud*, an anthem for soprano solo and chorus, which was published by Novello & Co. Ltd in that year.

the place for a festival of song – a place without noise or hurry, with
no distractions, no jarring note to spoil the harmony. It is said that
Richard Wagner chose Bayreuth as the spot for his theatre because
of its removedness from the distracting influences of great cities,
and one appreciates his reason when one stands in this peaceful old
Abbey churchyard and all the air vibrates with music.

The Abbey lends itself to such a function. From an acoustic point
of view it nearly equals Gloucester Cathedral. The chorus singers are
placed in the chancel stalls, the instrumentalists occupy the floor,
and the principal vocalists sit just within the rood-screen. This is
not an ideal arrangement, but rather one with which much fault can
be found. On the other hand, there are many points in the Abbey
at which the confined performers can be heard to all necessary
advantage, while a certain picturesqueness of grouping and
architectural effect pleases the eye. These smaller gatherings for the
enjoyment of pure and lofty music deserve all the encouragement
that can be given to them. Without the pretensions and importance
of great festivals, they perhaps do a better work by furthering sacred
art where, without such help, it might languish, and by raising public
conception of what festal services should be.

— 10 —

The Gloucester Three Choirs Festival (1901)

Time was taken by the forelock in making preparations for the 1901 Festival. The Committee began its work in August, 1900, a month before the Hereford Meeting took place, the chief reason for this early assembly being the question of new works. I pointed out at the time the mistake made by Festival Committees in inviting composers to produce new works at absurdly short notice. It generally resulted in a novelty being handed out to the chorus a few weeks, and sometimes only a few days before the performance, thereby making an adequate rendering quite impossible.

Invitations for new works were sent to Parry,[1] Lloyd,[2] Cowen,[3] Coleridge-Taylor,[4] Lee Williams[5] and myself. Luard-Selby and West were invited to write a new setting of the canticles and a new anthem respectively for the opening of the Festival.[6] Eventually other new compositions were added to the list – *The Forging of the Anchor*, Bridge; Symphonic Poem, *A Song in the Morning*, Bell; and a descriptive Ballade, *The Gates of Night*, Hervey; making a total of eleven new works by British composers. The programme also included Stanford's *Last Post*, Mackenzie's 'Procession of the Ark' from *The Rose of Sharon* (specially arranged for this Festival) and, in addition to other works by him, Elgar's *Cockaigne* overture, which was heard for the first time at a Philharmonic Concert in June of that year. A remarkable list for a Three Choirs Meeting in those days!

---

1   *The Soldier's Tent*, song with orchestra.
2   *The righteous live for evermore*, for eight-part unaccompanied chorus.
3   *Phantasy of Life and Love*, for orchestra.
4   *Idyll*, for orchestra.
5   *A Harvest Song*, for solo soprano and chorus.
6   Luard-Selby's canticles were his 'Second Service' in A, for solo soprano, chorus and orchestra. West's contribution, which he himself conducted, was his Festival Anthem *Lord, I have loved the habitation of Thy house*, for soprano and bass soloists, chorus, orchestra and organ.

81

We certainly went beyond the recommendation of the Festival Committee of 1895 that one new work *only* should be included in the programme, but our action was justified by the results. We had a greater number of Stewards than there had ever been at Gloucester; the amount available for the Charity was over £1,700 – a record up to that time – and the attendances exceeded those of the previous Festival by one thousand.

On receiving the invitation from the Stewards to write a work for the Festival I consulted my friend, Joseph Bennett, who, as is well known, had considerable experience and great gifts as a writer of libretti. His books are numerous, and amongst them are to be found at least three operas, some twelve oratorios and half a dozen cantatas. Who then could give better advice or help in such a matter? The fact that he was a Gloucestershire man was another attraction to me. His reply to my appeal was that he would put on his thinking-cap and would do all he could to provide me with the necessary book.

I had not long to wait, for within a few days it arrived. It was on the subject of the Disciples journeying to Emmaus, and 'Emmaus' was to be the title of the work. With the words in my possession I travelled to North Wales for a holiday, where I hoped to stay until the cantata was finished. The surroundings were so congenial and I became so interested in the subject that I finished the work within four weeks.

I took the first opportunity of going through it with Mr Bennett before submitting it to a publisher, and as it satisfied his critical ear I lost no time in placing it in the hands of Messrs. Novello & Co. Everything went smoothly until the programme was publicly announced in the early spring preceding the Festival. The final proofs had been passed, and I was about to score the work when I received crushing news from the publishers. They had had a communication from another composer to the effect that he had noticed in the programme that my new work was a setting of Mr Joseph Bennett's words entitled *Emmaus*. He went on to say that he had purchased these words from Mr Bennett some years previously.[7]

---

7   The other composer cannot have been Sir Walford Davies, since the text of his 1899 anthem *The Walk to Emmaus* (for tenor and bass soloists and chorus) is Biblical. The likelihood is that an unknown composer had reserved the right to set Bennett's text but that the composition itself never materialized.

It transpired that Bennett, when searching through his manuscripts for a subject for my work, came across some loose sheets of paper on which was written a scene entitled *At Emmaus*, and forgetting all about the former transaction sent them to me as suitable material for a Cantata.

In reply to a letter of distress from me Bennett wrote that he had been in many a worse mess and all would come right! He would re-write the words. This, however, entailed the re-writing of a great part of the music. When this difficulty had been surmounted we were within a few weeks of the Festival – the chorus had their part to learn and not a note had been scored.

I was seriously thinking of withdrawing it from the programme when I received the following letter from Elgar:

> Bettws-y-coed
> N. Wales
> June 14, 1901

My dear Brewer
    Good! If I *can* I'll conduct "Cockaigne" for you but you would do it all right if I cannot come. I'll look out for you in town next week.
    Jaeger – who has been in Malvern – but of course you know that – tells me by this post that you are somehow worried – (the exact *nuance* I don't quite understand – about getting your work ready) – he said something before we left home and I told him you must not be worried and that if necessary to make things smooth I would orchestrate some for you – that's all – I know it's a cheek to offer but if I can save you a little worry let me do so.

> Yours ever
> Edward Elgar

A more generous act could not be imagined. The proof copy of *Emmaus* was sent to him, and in a few days I received a letter which serves to prove the infinite trouble he took over the score:

> Malvern
> June 30, 1901

My dear Brewer
    I have scored Nos. 1, 4, 5, 6, 9 and 10. If that's not enough you must let me know. I send on my MS. I *hope* it

will please you but I feel much at sea as to your wishes and I am sadly afraid you will not like my interpretation – the Tuttis may be all right.

No. 1 – see p.7 of MS. (p.2 in vocal score). I *fattened* out the p.f. arrgt here – see strings especially last three bars, and on – you can easily sacrifice any of my orch: devices by a stroke of the pen.

I took the *bar before B* to be the actual "chord of climax" and worked up to that: hence the brass alone and cumulative effect 3rd bar 3rd line.

See Andante Moderato p.16 – I didn't know how much *force* you want and I have made you a fine burst, which will sound jolly but you may want to be more austere – It can easily be cut out.

p.17, line 2, I gave this wholly (except final chords) for strings – I don't think it wants *colour* but you may have meant it for *wind* – but I give the soft wind a chance (contrasting) at letter **R**.

At **O** are these chords what you want? or do you want strings? at **P** I have to carry on *the flow* of the parts added a few notes for Vio: I – knock 'em out if you like.

2 bars before **S**. I've stuck *c* in first Vio: to avoid clashing with vocal part – also in the *rall.* near end – I have carried celli down to A.

The harp is effective but *ad lib.*

Thinking you will use the organ in other more likely places I've not put it in except a ped: or two in Introduction.

I *have not* revised any of it I fear, as usual, there may be many errors but one of your pupils could look it thro': the first thing however is to know if it will *DO* at all for you.

Kind regards
Yours ever
Ed. Elgar

P.S. – I find I cannot send the parcel by post to-day: but will despatch it to-morrow. Send me a wire *in the a.m.* saying if you want me to continue any other numbers – *spell* the number (seven not 7) to avoid mistakes. If you are at liberty come over to see me, if necessary, and have lunch or something, let me hear if you are coming. I'm not let out on account of my chill.

I should be glad to see you. In haste.

A few days later he writes:

Malvern
July 7, 1901

My dear Brewer

I shall hope to despatch by an early post to-morrow the remainder of your score – it's all ready now but Sunday's a *dies non* with us as far as business posts are concerned.

I have taken great pleasure in trying to interpret your thoughts and feelings and only hope I have not grossly misrepresented them. Now: please *accept* my work on your score and never think I want any return whatever: keep a kind thought for a fellow sometime – that's all.

Please look very carefully thro' all the parts especially – once more – the transposing things.

I have enjoyed your themes immensely and they lend themselves to colour famously. I am especially pleased with No.7 and (as far as I am concerned) with the first part of No.11 – the end is good (as far as you're concerned) but I think you might have instrumented it better than I have.

I wish the work every success and if you have been saved any pin-pricks and have had a good rest I am happy in having done it!

Our kindest regards to you both.

Yours always
Edward Elgar

In the vocal score he writes

– Began June 27, 1901. Ended July 7, 1901.

What this unselfish act meant to me it is difficult to describe. It not only relieved me of an enormous amount of work at an anxious time, but the scoring of my work by the master hand has been an invaluable lesson to me, and I feel that what measure of success *Emmaus* has attained is largely due to the effective orchestration. When one considers the number of big works Elgar then had on hand, and the physical strain alone of the actual writing, one has some slight conception of the generosity of this most friendly act.

And here I would record my gratitude to Lady Elgar for her untiring energy in preparing the score for her husband to work upon – work behind the scenes, unknown, unrecognized, yet how valuable![8]

In spite of all these efforts to avoid the infringement of copyright the lawyers were not to be so appeased, and a week before the Festival we were warned that the performance of *Emmaus* would render us liable for heavy penalties. This cheering (!) news greeted me on my arrival in London for the rehearsals of soloists and orchestra. Madame Albani,[9] who was to be one of the soloists in the work, said that if imprisonment was to be the result, she would accompany me to prison! Legal interviews ensued, and permission was given for the work to be performed on condition that it was afterwards withdrawn and the plates destroyed. To such terms I naturally could not consent. The work must be given a chance to live or not be performed at all. Eventually, through the good auspices of Messrs. Novello, the claim was withdrawn and the work allowed to be published and performed.

The London orchestral rehearsals, coming as they do when little else is taking place in London, form a happy meeting-place for musicians and their friends. One of these visitors, in that particular year, was Sir August Manns,[10] who had done so much for the British composer at the Crystal Palace. The letter which he sent me during the Festival was encouraging and cheered me on.

Sep. 11 1901

Dear Sir

Let me offer you my best congratulations to the success of the opening concerts of the Gloucester Musical Festival, and to thank you at the same time heartily for your courtesy by sending me the particulars of the

---

8 Elgar's letters to Jaeger from late June and July 1901 say that he had "taken much joy" in working on the orchestration of *Emmaus*, and that his offer to help Brewer had been prompted by his concern over the health of Brewer and his wife. Elgar refused to accept any payment for his work. See Percy M. Young (ed.), *Letters to Nimrod: Edward Elgar to August Jaeger, 1897–1908* (London, 1965), pp.135–7.

9 Dame Emma Albani (1847–1930), Canadian-born soprano.

10 Sir August Manns (1825–1907), the German-born conductor, later took British citizenship. He conducted concerts at the Crystal Palace from 1855 to 1901.

rehearsals and the permission for me and Mrs. Manns to attend them.

Your Festival programmes are of high musical interest.

Hoping that unqualified success will reward your artistic efforts,

I remain
Yours sincerely
August Manns

These rehearsals, which in my early youth occupied one day, gradually grew from one day to two days until in 1904 a third day was requisitioned. But even that is insufficient in these modern times when Colour Symphonies[11] and such-like complex works have to be rehearsed.

After the final performance of the 1901 Festival I was presented by the Gloucester contingent of the chorus with my portrait, a gift which proved to me their friendship and affection.

It was at this Festival that a visitor wished to enter the Cathedral during one of the performances. On demanding admission he was told that he could not enter without a ticket. "Do you mean to tell me," he indignantly exclaimed, "that I shall require a ticket to enter the Kingdom of Heaven?" "Well, no," explained the polite Steward, "but you won't hear Madame Albani in Heaven!"

When the enormity of his remark dawned upon him that Steward turned and fled.

---

11 This is an undisguised reference to Sir Arthur Bliss's *Colour Symphony*, which received its first performance at the 1922 Gloucester Festival.

– 11 –

The founding of the Gloucestershire Orchestral Society (1901)

The Gloucester Choral Society, to which I have already referred, and which forms the nursery, so to speak, of the Festival chorus, had been doing good work for many years past, but had often found itself in financial difficulties in consequence of having to engage the assistance of a professional orchestra at each of its concerts. It was this fact that determined me to attempt to establish an orchestral society, and in June [1901] I wrote a letter to the press, bringing before the public the project which I had in mind – namely the formation of an orchestral society which should include in its membership not only players living in the city, but also those living in the outlying districts of the county.

I pointed out the possibility and the desirability of furthering the appreciation of music by bringing together in such a society the many lovers of music, both performers and non-performers, who had little or no opportunity of studying concerted works. I knew that scattered over the county were any number of musical enthusiasts anxious, not only to listen to music, but to take part in the performance of it. Such a society, I considered, would be the means of supplying a long-felt want to musical organizations all over the county. It would also provide opportunity for earnest amateur musicians to exercise those artistic abilities which, developed by expensive education, only too often languish through the absence of any inducement to continued culture. A meeting was accordingly called of the leading professional and amateur musicians of the neighbouring towns, who generously promised their support in time and money.

As this society is unique in its organization it may be of interest to the reader to know under what conditions it was established. It was decided to hold the full rehearsals in Gloucester. These, for the convenience of county members, were held in the afternoon, and arrangements were made with the railway companies for members, on presenting coupons at the ticket office, to make the double journey for a single fare and a quarter. It was also arranged to hold sub-centre practices at places where a sufficient number of members could attend to form a class. The members living in or near these sub-centres met for practice each week in which there was no *full* rehearsal, under the direction of a competent professional leader. By this means more detailed attention could be given to the rendering of the music than was possible at a full band practice, and those who had not had previous experience in orchestral playing found great advantage in studying in even smaller groups under capable instruction.

In order to obtain a competent professional instructor I corresponded with Sir Hubert Parry[1] and Sir Alexander Mackenzie[2] with a view to attracting a first-rate violinist who could give the necessary instruction, and also give private lessons to any who wished to continue their study of a stringed instrument. The enormous benefit to music in the county generally to be derived from such an arrangement will readily be seen.

Parry's reply was as follows:

> Royal College of Music
> Prince Consort Road
> South Kensington, London
> October 23, 1901

My dear Brewer

I am very glad to see the Orchestral Society is really on its legs, and I hope it will prosper.

I am afraid it will be very difficult to find the young violinist you describe. Our young violinists get such a lot of work to do in London that they won't venture into the provinces. We have had the greatest difficulty in even finding any one to take up good appointments in schools. I have racked my brains and made inquiries so far in vain.

I am afraid the only course I can think of is to look round in Bath or Bristol or Birmingham. A young man won't venture into a new district on such a chance ...

> Very sincerely yours
> C. Hubert H. Parry

---

1   Director of the Royal College of Music from 1895 to 1918.
2   Principal of the Royal Academy of Music from 1888 to 1924.

It was left to Mackenzie to find the young man who had the spirit of enterprise, and who was prepared to "venture into a new district on such a chance." A more thoroughly equipped musician could not have been found if this island of ours had been searched from Land's End to John o' Groats than Mackenzie's nominee.

The young man who "ventured into the provinces" was W. H. Reed, the present leader of the London Symphony Orchestra,[3] whose name is now not only a household word in the city and county of Gloucester, but who is known as a performer and composer throughout the length and breadth of the land. The good resulting from the influence and labours of such a highly gifted musician, performer and instructor, and from the untiring energy and perseverance which he devoted to an indescribably arduous and uphill task, cannot be exaggerated. Once a fortnight from October to Easter (the society's activities cease during the summer months) he visited Gloucestershire to direct rehearsals at the various centres.

Unfortunately – but naturally – his time became more and more taken up by important duties as Professor of the violin at the Royal College of Music and elsewhere, and he is now able to give but little attention to the Gloucestershire Orchestral Society. But the good seed sown by him is bearing fruit.

From the outset the movement was taken up with the greatest enthusiasm. Sir Hubert Parry became President. At the start some eighty members enrolled themselves as performers, and within a short time this number had increased to one hundred and fifty. The main difficulty we had to cope with was the lack of wind players. Having many articled pupils at the time of the society's inauguration I found it possible to fill several gaps with these young men. Two of them became excellent horn players. But the war, alas, robbed us of many useful performers including our invaluable secretary, B. V. Bruton, who was a first-rate amateur oboe player.[4]

We began with sub-centres in Tewkesbury, Stroud and Berkeley in addition to Gloucester, but within a very short time we had added

---

3 Reed joined the LSO in 1904, becoming its leader in 1912.
4 Capt. Basil Vassar Bruton (1878–1918), Adjutant of the 1/5th Battalion Gloucestershire Regiment, was killed on 15 June 1918 at Asiago Plateau on the Italian Front. His name is included on a War Memorial in St Catharine's Church, Gloucester. Curiously, Brewer does not mention that Bruton was his brother-in-law.

Cheltenham, Tetbury, Frampton and Newnham to the list. The ranks of this huge orchestra were recruited from all classes, the strings being drawn largely from the fair sex and numbering over one hundred players.

As to the programmes carried out by the Society since it blossomed into existence I can, of course, only indicate their character. It has performed most of the symphonies of Beethoven, Mozart, Schumann, Brahms, Schubert, Dvořák and Tchaikovsky, and in association with the Choral Society the majority of the big classics, as well as the great works by modern composers. Parry often expressed his astonishment at the high standard reached at the concerts, and I have more than once been asked by the uninitiated whether I contemplated using the Society at the Festival! The Society has more than fulfilled its purpose. Its members are called upon for assistance at concerts all over the county wherever choral works are performed and an orchestra is required, and but for its assistance the Gloucester Choral Society could not afford to have an orchestra at each of its concerts. *The Daily Telegraph*, in commenting on the Society's work, says:

> Could not Dr Brewer be persuaded to bring his amateur orchestra – those 150 Gloucestershire enthusiasts – to Queen's Hall in order that Londoners might enjoy a taste of their quality? Surely such an experience would be, like the Society itself, unique.

I have dwelt at length on the work of the Society because I am firmly convinced that such an organization advances the appreciation and standard of music enormously. I hope many such societies may be established throughout the country. But it must not be imagined that good results are easily obtained. Training an amateur society of this kind is often heartrending work, and a man must be prepared to face enormous difficulties and persevere in surmounting them. The conducting of a professional orchestra is, by comparison, child's play. But the strenuous work is often relieved by amusing incidents. On one occasion we were rehearsing Dvořák's *New World* Symphony for the first time, and the second bassoon looked sorely troubled and perplexed when we began the slow movement. The movement is in D flat, and the bassoons in the first bar have to play B natural and E natural. My friend, the second bassoon, failed to play the first note, and I asked him the reason of his silence. Scratching his head and looking thoroughly bewildered he said: "I think there must be something wrong with my copy. It begins with an accidental!"

It was at the annual general meeting of the Gloucester Orchestral Society in 1921 that I dwelt at some length on the activities of the Three Choirs Festivals and what they had done for music in England. The question had often been asked as to which was the most musical spot in England. Some said it was to be found in the north. Others said that the centre of all things musical was London. But I claimed that it was not in the north nor yet in London, but it was to be found within a radius of thirty miles of Gloucester Cathedral. It embraced, of course, the sister cathedral cities of Worcester and Hereford. Here in this small compass existed one of the oldest, if not *the* oldest, musical institution – the Three Choirs Festivals. Festivals had been held in the past at Birmingham, Norwich, Leeds, Sheffield, and other big centres, but they were always held triennially. In this district these great historic meetings were held annually in cities of only a moderate size with an average population of about 40,000. They had already been in existence about forty years when Bach and Handel died. It was an extraordinary achievement to have carried them on so successfully for now over 200 years.[5] It is difficult to imagine what would have happened to the oratorio but for these festivals. It would not be an exaggeration to say that they had greatly helped to keep this form of composition alive. Composers had had the opportunity of hearing their works performed under such conditions as were impossible in any other place. In addition to these yearly Festivals there were some twenty-five musical societies flourishing within this radius, which was an astounding fact.

There was also the creative talent that had sprung from this small area. We could claim the greatest musical genius of the age – Sir Edward Elgar. Here too lived Parry and S. S. Wesley. The latter perhaps did more for church music than any other composer since the Elizabethan period. Then there were also Lloyd and Hayes[6] and

---

5   The origins of the Three Choirs Festival can be traced to the early 18th century. See Boden, p.1.

6   William Hayes (1708–77) was a chorister at Gloucester Cathedral. He was Organist of Magdalen College, Oxford, from 1734 until his death.

others whose names were familiar. The modern school of composers was well represented too. We could claim Vaughan Williams, Holst, Harrison,[7] Howells, and quite an array of other young men, the like of whom were not to be found in so limited a space elsewhere.[8] In addition this area had produced executants, singers and musical critics who had become world famous, and last but not least Sir Henry Hadow, the greatest living writer on the art of music.[9]

On these grounds I claimed that within that specified area was the most musical spot of the empire. My remarks gave rise to a storm of criticism in the London press and elsewhere, some abusing me and others admitting that I had some justification for my claim. One paper gave vent to the following caustic and cutting remark, "Are we not right in supposing that Dr Brewer is organist there?"

---

7   Julius Harrison (1885–1963), who was born in Worcestershire, achieved some renown as an operatic composer and conductor. Some of his compositions show the influence of his teacher Granville Bantock.
8   Brewer might also have mentioned Ivor Gurney (1890–1937), a war poet and an outstanding composer of songs, who had become a chorister in the Cathedral choir at the age of nine, and who – like Herbert Howells and Ivor Novello – had been one of his articled pupils. Gurney's exclusion may be due to the stigma which then attached to the mental illness from which he suffered throughout his life.
9   See above, p.23, fn.20.

– 12 –

1904–6

Once again, no sooner was the Hereford Meeting at an end in 1903 than we turned our thoughts to the necessary preparation for the 1904 Festival at Gloucester. The Stewards at their first meeting invited Sir Hubert Parry to write a new work, and the short oratorio, *The Love that casteth out Fear*, was the outcome of the invitation. At the same time the Stewards expressed a wish that a new composition from my pen should be included in the scheme. I again sought the advice of Joseph Bennett. The 'book' which he provided dealt with Herod and the massacre of the children. These were the only two works decided on in the early stages, but eventually no fewer than seven new compositions were produced. In the programme which was submitted to the committee I had included *The Dream of Gerontius* and *The Apostles*. The Dean, Dr Spence-Jones, said that it was impossible to allow *The Dream of Gerontius* to be sung in Gloucester Cathedral without the process of expurgation being applied in certain instances. Although I pointed out that the work had been sung at Hereford and Worcester with some emendations, he would not be convinced of its fitness, so I had to be satisfied on this occasion with an excerpt from this immortal work – 'The Prelude and Angel's Farewell'. It was not until 1910 that *The Dream of Gerontius* was given in its entirety at Gloucester.[1] The inclusion of *The Apostles* in the scheme proved an enormous success from every point of view. The work was produced at the Birmingham Festival the previous year and this was the first performance at a Three Choirs Festival. It drew the largest attendance of the week, no less than four hundred more than *Elijah*, and over three hundred more than the *Messiah*. The collection for the Charity was also considerably greater than at either performance of the older works. W. H. Reed's name appeared for the first time as a composer at this Meeting, through the inclusion of his *Scenes from the Ballet*.

---

1   Dean Spence-Jones had clearly relented, as he remained in office until his death in 1917.

94

No difficulties arose this year over the production of my work, *The Holy Innocents*. Mr Bennett forwarded the libretto to me in parts as he wrote it, and this time I knew that portions of it had not been discovered at the bottom of a drawer.[2] I was able, therefore, to get the work well in hand. When the time came for its performance, not only did the chorus give of their best towards the end of a very heavy week, but I was well served with my soloists – a better cast could not have been found in those days – Madame Albani, Miss Muriel Foster, Mr John Coates,[3] Mr Ffrangcon-Davies[4] and Mr Dalton Baker.[5] This was, I regret to say, the last appearance of those gifted artists, Madame Albani and Miss Muriel Foster, at a Gloucester Festival, for before the next one took place in 1907 they had retired from the profession.[6]

The year following, 1905, the Archbishop of Canterbury[7] conferred on me the degree of Doctor of Music. The ceremonial took place at Lambeth Palace on May 20. Amongst the many letters of congratulation which I received was the following from Sir Hubert Parry:

> Royal College of Music
> March 25, 1905

> My dear Brewer
>   Last night I received a note from Lambeth Palace,
> containing such very pleasing news that I must write

---

2   See above, pp.82–6, for the copyright problems which Brewer experienced over the libretto for *Emmaus*.

3   John Coates (1865–1941) is particularly remembered for having been a soloist (again with Muriel Foster) in the successful 1902 Worcester Festival performance of *The Dream of Gerontius*, which redeemed the work following its disastrous 1900 Birmingham premiere. He also performed in Elgar's *The Apostles* and *The Kingdom*, and in Granville Bantock's *Omar Khayyám* at the Birmingham Festivals of 1903, 1906 and 1909 respectively.

4   David Ffrangcon-Davies (1855–1918) was a Welsh operatic baritone, and father of the actress Dame Gwen Ffrangcon-Davies (1891–1992).

5   William Henry ('Dalton') Baker (1879–1970), English baritone, emigrated to Canada in 1914.

6   Brewer's memory may have been playing tricks here. According to Boden, p.153, Muriel Foster performed several demanding roles in the 1912 Hereford Festival, following which she retired.

7   The then Archbishop, Randall Davidson (1848–1930), was Primate from 1903 to 1928. He was the first holder of the post to retire, all his predecessors having died in office.

to express my heartiest satisfaction thereat. It is a good thing to keep up the standard of that particular Degree by conferring it upon people who are likely to enhance its prestige, and your record so far has not only thoroughly justified the conferment but begets confidence that you will make the honour more honourable by the way you wear it.

Please give my love and congratulations to Mrs. Brewer and the boy.[8] I'm sure they will be pleased, and so will Gloucester in general.

Yours very sincerely and pleasedly
C. Hubert H. Parry

In the Chapter House of the Cathedral on July 15 Dean Spence-Jones, on behalf of the Stewards of the Festival, subscribers and members of the Festival Class, the Gloucester Choral, Orpheus and Orchestral Societies, presented me with the Mus. Doc. robes, an illuminated address, and a cheque as a mark of appreciation of the honour conferred on me by the Archbishop of Canterbury.[9]

The title of 'Dr' has often led to amusing episodes, and I cannot refrain from relating one which happened at a London hotel. My wife and I were having breakfast when a lady, who was sitting at a table behind us, fell back in a fit. My wife rushed to her assistance and accompanied her when she was carried from the room, and told the head waiter to summon a doctor immediately. Presently he came to my table and asked if I was Dr Brewer. I replied in the affirmative, and he went on to say that he was sorry to disturb me, but there was a lady in a fit outside and could I attend to her at once! When I explained to him that I was not the kind of doctor who relieved pain, but, on the contrary, often inflicted it, he walked away and left the impression on my mind that he had a very poor opinion of my sort! Shortly after the conferring of the Doctor's degree the distinction

---

8   Parry's reference to 'the boy' is puzzling, since the Brewers had two young sons at the time – Charles Herbert (9) and Godfrey Noel (4).

9   Brewer's doctoral robes passed after his death to Herbert Sumsion (his pupil from 1914 to 1917 and his assistant from 1919 to 1922), who received the Lambeth D.Mus degree in 1947. They were subsequently worn by Sumsion's former assistant and successor, John Sanders (1933–2003), who received the Lambeth D.Mus degree in 1990.

of Honorary Membership of the Royal Academy of Music was conferred on me by the directors, an honour I greatly appreciated.

There is a lighter side to the Festivals the outside world knows little about. Who knows how John Coates and W. H. Reed fooled some hundreds of people outside the Cathedral at Worcester before the *Messiah* performance one Friday morning? It happened in this way. They were both staying with me, as they usually do when the Festival is away from Gloucester, and in the drawing-room of the house which I had taken for the week was a brass hearth-brush, which looked uncommonly like a large telescope. Reed, on catching sight of it, exclaimed, "What an excellent thing for a practical joke!" They immediately proceeded to action, and took up their position outside the house in College Yard, and appeared to look through this imaginary telescope at the tower of the Cathedral. Very soon a huge crowd of people collected round them trying to discover what it was they were watching so intently. It was a bright, cloudless day, and the glare from the sun made it difficult for the people to look at the tower, and the male portion of the crowd tilted their hats over their eyes, and even the police who were on duty were anxious to discover the object of interest. This continued for several minutes, the traffic meanwhile becoming very congested. Then Reed suggested to Coates that it was time for the crowd to see the business end of the hearth brush. When they saw the bristles appear and spread out at the end of the brass tube and realized how they had been fooled there was a roar of laughter, the crowd rapidly dispersed, and the serious-minded Festival goers proceeded on their way to the Cathedral.

It was for the Hereford Festival of 1906 that I wrote the first set of *Elizabethan Pastorals* for John Coates to sing at the secular concert. He brought his great artistic powers into play, and made them an instantaneous success. Another tenor had been engaged to sing in *Elijah* at this Meeting of the Three Choirs, and so John Coates had a day off. But not being of an idle nature he occupied his time in other ways that morning. I had taken a house in the corner of the Close – Harley Court. There was a passageway in front of it leading from the Close to another part of the town. To the surprise of Herefordians and visitors to the Festival they saw, on leaving the Cathedral for the luncheon interval, some notice boards in front of my house which had not been there earlier in the day. One was placed on a privet hedge warning people "not to pluck the flowers". On a few blades of grass and weeds was another, advising people to "keep off the sward", and on a door leading to a rubbish heap near the house was the following notice – "You are requested not to feed the wild Zigmollicans". It was highly amusing to watch these well-dressed people walk on tiptoe to the door and peer over cautiously, expecting to see some kind of wild beast in a pen; and then, on discovering only a heap of dead leaves, slink away, casting furtive glances around to see if their action had been observed.

The *Musical Times*[10] of the following month commented on the incident thus:

> Much interest was aroused at Hereford by some specimens of that rare animal, the Zigmollicon [*sic*]. They were kept in confinement by an eminent brewer residing near the cathedral, and passers by who managed to catch a glimpse of the elusive little creatures greatly admired their subtly-tinted coats. It was reported that they had been recently imported by Herr Johann von Ueberrock, the well-known zoological specialist!

One more Coates story. This time the scene was laid at Worcester. A small choirboy approached him and asked as a special favour if he would be so kind as to write his name in his autograph book. John Coates, who had been signing autograph books continually during the week, said to the boy: "Haven't I done so already, my boy? Just look." The boy proceeded to turn the pages backwards and forwards and then, looking up, said quite innocently, "Let me see, sir, what is your name?"!

---

10 In one of only two footnotes in his *Memories* Brewer attributes this to 'Dr Herbert Thompson', music and art critic of the *Yorkshire Post* from 1886 to 1936, though the original report in *Musical Times*, 47 (1906), p.675, is unattributed. Brewer spells the creature 'Zigmollican', perhaps a slip. The references to 'brewer' and 'coats' speak for themselves. The terminal exclamation mark is Brewer's.

– 13 –

1907–10

The year 1907 was a busy one for me. In addition to an invitation for a new work from the Gloucester Stewards, I received commissions from the authorities at Leeds and Cardiff to write for their Festivals. As there was some difficulty in finding a suitable libretto, I had to give up all thoughts of writing a work for my own Festival, and *Emmaus* was inserted in the programme instead. For Leeds I wrote *In Springtime*, Pastorals for solo tenor and male voice chorus, and for Cardiff a choral setting of the ballad, *Sir Patrick Spens*. There were only two novelties in the Gloucester programme, *Christ in the Wilderness*, by Granville Bantock, and Scherzo Fantastique, *Caliban*, by W. H. Reed. Neither Sir Hubert Parry nor Richard Strauss, both of whom had been invited to write, were able to provide new works. Although many novelties were not produced we were fortunate in being able to include in the programme *The Kingdom*, which had been heard for the first time at the Birmingham Festival the previous year. It was performed on the Wednesday morning, and proved a great attraction. *The Apostles* had been given the evening before. I trust that some day it may fall to the lot of Gloucester to produce the complete trilogy from the master mind.[1]

In the same programme as *The Kingdom* was included Glazunov's Symphony in C minor (No.6).[2] I was anxious to induce the distinguished Russian to come and conduct the work, but the reason of his inability to do so is set forth in the following letter:[3]

---

1 The first occasion on which all three of Elgar's oratorios were performed at the same festival was at the Worcester Festival of 1984, under the Gloucester-born conductor Dr Donald Hunt.
2 Granville Bantock's *Christ in the Wilderness*, too, was included in this same concert (11 September 1907).
3 Glazunov's Symphony No.6 was conducted by Brewer himself.

St. Petersburg
Kasansnage 10
6 August 1907

(Translation)

My dear Sir

I have just returned from St Petersburg, where I received your letter of July 11th. I consider your proposal that I should conduct at the Gloucester Musical Festival a great honour, but unfortunately can only leave St Petersburg in the summer, as I am tied there as Director of the Conservatorium.

It is just in September that the work of the Conservatorium begins and my presence then is very important.

I regret very much that it is not possible for me to return to England and remain gratefully and with kindest regards

Alexander Glazunov

Although there were fewer Stewards at this Festival there was no lack of enthusiasm for – or support of – the Meeting. The attendance was nearly 3,000 more than in 1904, and there was also an increase in the collections, the sum available for the Charity amounting to nearly £1,700. It is of interest to record that on this occasion a solo violinist performed in the Cathedral for the first time at a Three Choirs Festival. Mischa Elman was specially engaged to play Beethoven's *Romance in F* at the Thursday evening performance, and made a profound impression.[4]

The work which I had written for the Cardiff Festival was *Sir Patrick Spens* for baritone solo, chorus and orchestra. The Chorus proved to be an excellent body of singers, full of vitality and freshness, and as I had had the opportunity of rehearsing the work on more than one occasion with them apart from the orchestra, we were able to get to know each other, and my expectations were more than realized by a capital performance. That great artist, Ffrangcon-

---

4   Elman also played Beethoven's Violin Concerto at the concert on the previous evening.

Davies, whose early death was a sad loss to the musical world, sang the part of Sir Patrick.[5]

The following month (October) saw the production of my Pastorals, *In Springtime*, for tenor solo and male voice chorus at Leeds, Gervase Elwes being responsible for the solo part. An amusing paragraph headed 'Wealthy Organists' appeared in a Leeds paper during the Festival week. The paragraph began by saying that "Organists in the West are looked upon as men of wealth." I tried to imagine that the writer meant wealth of musical ideas, but I'm afraid such meaning was far from his thoughts. The paragraph continues:

> Dr Brewer is as good a judge of investments as he is of music. He has for neighbour Sir Hubert Parry, who can afford to entertain on a lavish scale in connection with the Festival at Gloucester Cathedral – and he is an organist also. It is clear that notes of music are not the only notes to which these musicians give their attention.

I might add that it is a noteworthy fact that Sir Hubert never at any time of his busy life held an organist's appointment. It is true that Parry entertained on what was certainly not a minor scale, but the scribe of Leeds was wrong in his other surmises![6]

For the Worcester Festival in 1908 I set W. E. Henley's inspiring poem, *England, my England*, which was sung by Plunket Greene[7] at the secular concert. It was one of two works specially written for this Festival, the other also coming from Gloucestershire – *Beyond these voices there is peace*, by Parry. It is interesting to recall that the poet W. E. Henley was also a Gloucester boy.[8]

Hubert Parry was ever ready to help in all musical projects in Gloucester. He possessed the same generous spirit as his father,

---

5   David Ffrangcon-Davies died in 1918 at the age of 68.
6   Brewer was perhaps being a little disingenuous here. When his estate was assessed for probate in April 1928 its value was given as £20,737 13s. 5d, a considerable sum in those days. For his widow's assessment of Brewer's financial astuteness and of his business acumen see below, pp.175–6.
7   Harry Plunket Greene (1865–1936), Irish baritone best known for his interpretation of English songs and German lieder.
8   William Ernest Henley (1849–1903) had been a pupil at The Crypt Grammar School, Gloucester.

and became one of Gloucester's benefactors by enlarging the Shire Hall, and thereby giving extra seating accommodation for about three hundred people. Not only musicians have benefited by his munificence, but the citizens generally have now the advantage of possessing a hall for meetings of all descriptions which will seat a thousand people.[9]

The enlarging of the Shire Hall had been a project long dear to his heart and ever in his mind. He discussed it with me and corresponded on the subject many times before it became an actual fact. Early in May, 1907, he asks: "What is happening about the construction of the orchestra in the Shire Hall? I stand by my offer of £200 if anything practical can be done. I hope it has not been shelved." I then made other suggestions to which he replied, "But if such a big job is to be undertaken it won't be ready by the Festival time. Is there anything else could be done to make the Shire Hall more serviceable? How about clearing away those vile sideway seats, and bringing all the floor to a level? I believe the estimate was about £90. If you don't want any contribution to the orchestra it might go to that." Later he writes:

> I am sorry nothing has been attainable about the Shire Hall. I hope we shall be able to go at it earlier next time and get something really complete done in the intervening years before 1910.

I should explain that the Shire Hall is under the control of the County Council. The County Surveyor at the time was either not in sympathy with the scheme or could not see his way to sanction the alterations; anyhow nothing was done. True to his word Sir Hubert began to take up the question of reconstruction in all seriousness before the end of 1909. In November of that year he again wrote to me on the subject:

> If the alterations are made at the street end we can get no more than ten feet extension of the room, and I very much doubt if the rebuilding can be done for £1,500 or that it will be worth the money when it is done. I can't help thinking

---

9   The Shire Hall in Westgate Street, designed by Sir Robert Smirke, was opened in 1816.

something might be done at the other end. The staircase and staircase lobby appear to me to be very wasteful in space and to admit of rearrangement, I am very anxious to do it before next Festival, and hoped to scrape the money together, and I have made £1,000 available – and then I get a check, for Highnam spire has come to grief and I have got to rebuild the top of it. This may make the provision of the additional £500 very difficult. But I am prepared to have a try at it if the reconstruction could be done for the money. If it can't how would it be to do away with the vile old orchestral platform and put a proper one, and improve the Hall otherwise by removing the raised seats at the side? It would at least make the place more decent; and I think it could be done for £1,000.

Here was a man with practical ideas that had not occurred to the architect. The outcome of this correspondence was that I attended a Committee meeting of the Council to explain Sir Hubert's plans with regard to the orchestra. The design he wished to see carried out was similar to the one at the Royal College of Music, and this he proposed should be built in front of the organ, which was of massive structure and occupied floor space.[10] The Chairman pointed out that if this scheme were carried through, considerably more floor space would have to be given up, and as this was of vital importance they did not see how they could accept Sir Hubert's most generous offer (which by then had been increased to £1,500), unless some other scheme could be devised.

I was loath to give up the idea of improving the Hall. Then a happy thought struck me – why not scrap the old organ, carry out Sir Hubert's design for the orchestra and build a new organ over it? On making this suggestion I was met with the obvious and practical remark, "Who is going to be responsible for the money for the new instrument?" I then told them that if the meeting could be adjourned for a fortnight I might be in a position to answer their question. This they consented to do.

---

10 The original organ, dating from 1849/50, was built by the Worcester organ builder John Nicholson. Its history is described in Roy Williamson, *The Organs of Gloucester, Tewkesbury and Cirencester, from the XVth Century* (Cheltenham, 1991), pp.84–7.

Before the next meeting I had written to my friends explaining the position, and their replies were so satisfactory that I was able to tell the Committee that I would be responsible for the new organ. Within the year I had collected the necessary amount by subscriptions and giving recitals on the new organ.[11] The County Surveyor's services at this juncture were invaluable. Colonel Sinnott entered into the movement wholeheartedly, and was able to see the result of his labours carried out without a hitch and the work completed in time for the Festival.[12]

At the secular concert of the Festival the Mayor presented Sir Hubert Parry with an address of gratitude for his generous gift for the enlarging and improvement of the Hall, which Sir Hubert acknowledged with a speech in which he tried characteristically to persuade the audience that most of the thanks were due to other people. I had hoped that the gratitude of the city would take a more tangible form, and that the Freedom of the City would have been conferred on Sir Hubert. I took steps to bring this about, but unfortunately Parry's political views were very pronounced, and he had recently appeared on the political platform and spoken in no uncertain voice. Party feeling, alas, runs very high in Gloucester, as in most cathedral cities, and, as these views did not coincide with those of the party in power at the time, I was unable to achieve my project and secure this recognition of Parry's munificence.

When I had completed my task of collecting the money for the organ Sir Hubert wrote:

Royal College of Music
Nov. 17 1910

My dear Brewer
    That's splendid! I congratulate you on the achievement. You are a perfect marvel at getting subscriptions. And it is delightful to hear of the audiences at your organ Recitals.

---

11 The replacement instrument of 1910 was built by Norman and Beard. See *BIOS REPORTER*, January 1992, Vol.16 No.1. Parry's obituary in *Musical Times*, 59 (1918), pp.489–91, refers to an impressive speech given by him at the inauguration of the organ. The instrument was removed in 1958 to Punshon Memorial Methodist Church, Bournemouth.

12 Colonel Edward Stockley Sinnott (1868–1969) was County Surveyor for Gloucestershire from 1907 to 1935, and was a noted local benefactor.

Just the very thing to make the whole affair complete. It is a joy to think of the Hall coming in so useful, and in such a right way. And I hope it will lead to the public supporting Concerts in Crowds too!

Yours very sincerely
C. Hubert H. Parry

This year's Festival was marked by other features in addition to the enlarging of the Shire Hall. Five new works were produced in the following order – *Fantasia on a Theme by Thomas Tallis* (for string orchestra), Vaughan Williams;[13] *Concerto for Organ and Orchestra in D major*, Basil Harwood; *The Lord's Prayer* (unaccompanied motet), C. Lee Williams; *Summer Sports* (suite for chorus and orchestra), A. H. Brewer, performed at the Shire Hall concert by the Gloucester contingent of the chorus; and 'Gethsemane' (an episode from *The Life of Christ*), Granville Bantock. At the performance in the Cathedral when the last named was produced, Fritz Kreisler gave a superb rendering of Bach's Violin Concerto in E. It was probably a unique experience for him to hear his own footsteps as he walked off the platform in silence after playing. During the performance of the Bach his E string broke and W. H. Reed immediately handed Kreisler his own instrument. When Reed had put a new string on Kreisler's violin he handed it to Kreisler, who refused it and continued to use Reed's. It afterwards transpired that the two instruments were twins – both being made by Joseph Guarnerius.

It was at this Festival that Reed first appeared as leader of the orchestra. The following year he was engaged to lead at the Handel Festival, and now there is hardly a Festival of note held in the country at which he does not lead. The Festival opened with Sullivan's *In Memoriam* Overture in memory of King Edward VII. The King had given his patronage to these historic Meetings since the Gloucester Festival of 1880.

---

13 In what must be regarded as a rare lapse of judgment Brewer described the 'Tallis Fantasia' to Herbert Howells as "a queer, mad work by an odd fellow from Chelsea". Although Howells, too, initially regarded it as "a strange work" he later came to regard it as "a supreme commentary by one great composer upon another". See Boden, pp.148–9.

– 14 –

Examining, adjudicating, and other anecdotes

It has been my privilege from time to time to meet many people of note who have visited the Cathedral at Gloucester. One of the first was the popular novelist, Miss Marie Corelli,[1] who was greatly interested in a violin *Romance* which I had recently published,[2] and which was written on the subject of her book, *Thelma*. On another occasion Sir H. Rider Haggard,[3] who was then occupied in writing his book, *Rural England*, visited Gloucester. It was in order to obtain material for this book that he was travelling through various parts of the country. Having gleaned the agricultural information he required from my father-in-law[4] he could not leave Gloucester without seeing the Cathedral. He expressed his great admiration for the building, and said it was one of the most splendid fanes[5] that he had seen in all his travels.[6] He was greatly amused with two stories in connection with the Cathedral which he introduced into his book, and which I venture now to repeat.

Some members of a Mothers' club from one of the Gloucester parishes, under the guidance of their vicar, visited the Cathedral. After these good women had been told what the monks did, and shown where the monks prayed, and amongst other things the famous lavatory of the monks, one old lady remained behind and, on shaking hands with the vicar, said she could appreciate all he had

---

1 Marie Corelli (1855–1924). The fullest account of her work is T. F. G. Coates and R. S. Warren Bell, *Marie Corelli: The Writer and the Woman* (Philadelphia, 1903).
2 *Romance in F* for Violin and Piano (Edwin Ashdown, [1896]).
3 Sir Henry Rider Haggard (1856–1925), author of adventure novels and other writings.
4 Brewer's father-in-law was Henry William Bruton (1843–1920), of the Gloucester firm of auctioneers and valuers Bruton Knowles & Co. His brother, Sir James Bruton, was Mayor of Gloucester at the outbreak of the First World War, and was MP for Gloucester from 1918 to 1923. There is a memorial to H. W. Bruton in Gloucester Cathedral.
5 i.e. churches.
6 *Rural England* was published in 1902. Haggard recounts his meeting with Brewer on p.396.

said about the monks much more than the other women "because you see, sir, it's like this, my old mother used to wash for them Monks." The "washing" to which that grateful old body referred was that of Bishop Monk, who held the See from 1830 to 1856! The other was the story of a verger taking a party of visitors round the Cathedral. As the reader is probably aware, the Cathedral is the birthplace of the Perpendicular style of architecture. When the party had reached the Choir, the guide informed them that "this 'ere style of archeetecture is what they call 'Perpindiculer' and that there," pointing to the Nave, "is what they call 'Norman'. This 'ere was put up first." A lady who was in the party said, "Excuse me, but aren't you making a mistake? Didn't the Norman period come first?" "Ah!" answered the undefeated verger, "that may be so in some places, but down 'ere they always 'ad a way o' their own!" Many stories might be told of these worthy custodians. I remember one complaining to me that he was so tied in the Cathedral that he was hardly ever able to go to a place of worship, and when he did go he liked to "take" his religion "a bit melancholy"!

Some years ago a deputation from this body of men waited on me just before one of my organ recitals. They had difficulty in opening the proceedings. They stood in a row in front of me – No.1 nudged No.2 to indicate that he was to start, but he was too bashful and so nudged No.3, who had the feeling, apparently, that his heart was in his mouth, and all that he could do was to nudge No.4. In a hoarse whisper No.4 gasped out, "Vittles is dearer!" From this I gathered that an increase of fee for the recitals would be acceptable to these loyal workers. I took the hint. All the vergers took a keen interest in the recitals. One of them, when wishing me "good night", would always add, "Quite a nice company here tonight, sir."!

At one time there were two Archdeacons in Gloucester who were residentiary Canons – Archdeacon S. and Archdeacon H. Archdeacon S., during Evensong one afternoon, discovered that he had left his glasses at his house, and as he had to read the First Lesson and couldn't see to read without them he asked the senior verger to go across to his study and fetch his glasses, which he was told he would find in the centre drawer of his writing-table. The verger failed to appear again in time for the First Lesson, and another Canon had to take the Archdeacon's place at the lectern. When Archdeacon H. returned to his house at the close of the service his study presented the appearance of an earthquake. He found that every conceivable thing had been turned out of his writing-table drawers and scattered all over the room! It appeared that when the verger left the Cathedral he quite forgot which Archdeacon had sent him for his glasses, and instead of going to Archdeacon S.'s house he invaded the other Archdeacon's study, with the foregoing disastrous result.

The following story of a Gloucester verger shows that he had his own views with regard to music. When he lay dying he sent a message to my predecessor asking for the 'Dead March' to be played at his funeral – *not* the "cock-a-doodle-do" one, but the one for which the blowers had to take off their coats and vests in order to keep the wind in, and in which the drums rolled! The cockadoodle one was evidently the middle section of the Funeral March from Beethoven's Sonata for the piano in A flat.[7] The late Dean (Dr Spence-Jones) used to delight in telling the story of how he took a party of American visitors round the Cathedral, which he loved so well. They, not knowing who their guide was, mistook him for a verger, and on departing tipped him a shilling. When telling me the story he said he valued that shilling more than any he had ever earned.

The life of an adjudicator at competition musical festivals is full of varied experiences, and the judge is exposed to as much criticism as he himself expends on the competitors. I have judged at most of the competition festivals throughout the country, and have had the experience of hearing hundreds of miners – friends and foes alike – sing "For he's a jolly good fellow" after hearing my decision. On the other hand I have been asked if I would like to know "the back way out!" On that particular occasion there were about ten thousand people present,[8] and when the secretary put this question to me before the competition commenced, I failed to grasp his meaning. I asked him to explain, and he informed me that, at their last competition, the two adjudicators had had to escape through the back door; a four-wheeler was waiting for them, and these

---

7   Sonata No.12 (Op.26).
8   It is difficult to imagine any festival venue that could have accommodated such a large number.

distinguished men were put on the floor of the cab and covered up with rugs, and that was how they had escaped to the station!

I think the most severe task I ever had at a competition festival was when I had to listen to Chopin's *Ballade in G minor* fifty-five times! We began at ten o'clock in the morning and did not finish until twelve hours later. One remembers the stories of early martyrdom, and one wonders why it was reserved for the twentieth century – the alleged age of philanthropy – to discover a torture which, for subtle and exquisite agony, puts all the old instruments of torture into the shade. On another occasion I had to listen to sixty contraltos sing *There is a bower of roses*.[9] When giving my decision on this class, I could not refrain from saying that I realized that it was a good song, but I now knew that bower of roses and I never wished to hear it again. A voice from the audience shouted, "Won't you sing it, sir?" "No," I replied, "I should be on *thorns* if I did!"

There was another occasion on which I must confess to having been guilty of a worse offence; I had finished my day's work, and I decided that I would like to hear my colleagues give some adjudications. Accordingly I sought out Hall No.1 but drew a blank – my friend in that room had also finished. Off I went to Hall No.2. There I had better luck. The judge was giving his decisions on the last class of the day. I sat myself down behind two very charming-looking young ladies and heard the following conversation in reference to the judge:

"Isn't he a darling?"

"Oh, isn't he a duck?"

"I wonder who he is?"

They had not got a programme and, hearing a movement behind them, they turned and appealed to me, and asked if I could tell them who the adjudicator was. The opportunity of doing myself a good turn was not to be lost, so I promptly replied, "I think it must be Dr Brewer!"

A musical examiner's experiences are also full of amusing incidents. Many stories might be told, and the following is certainly worth repeating. The daughter of a country vicar in the North of England thought she had discovered a wonderful prodigy. She took him in hand and gave him piano lessons, and decided after a time to

---

9   From Charles Villiers Stanford's first opera, *The Veiled Prophet of Khorassan*.

send him in for an elementary examination in music. The music was prepared and the great day arrived when he was to face an examiner for the first time. To give him confidence she accompanied her pupil to the scene of action, intending to sit in the room during the examination. She soon discovered, however, that this was against all rules. "Never mind," said she to the boy, "I will listen *outside* the door." Again she was informed that that was not allowed, and she was conducted to the waiting-room where she remained until the examination was over.

"Well," she greeted him on the completion of his task, "and how did you get on?"

"Oh, splendidly."

"Ear tests all right?"

"All correct."

"What about the scales?"

"Oh, I romped through them."

"And how did you get on with the pieces?"

"Oh, I played them through without a mistake."

"Then you must have got honours," exclaimed the proud teacher.

"Certain," replied the youth, "but, oh Miss, there is something wrong with that examiner; I think he must be suffering from some kind of religious mania. Do you know what he was doing all the time I was playing? He was holding his head in his hands and rocking himself to and fro exclaiming, 'O my God! O my God!'"

It is a fortunate thing that musicians, as a rule, have a keen sense of humour. It is often their salvation. At a festival not so long ago, a work was produced, the music being intended to depict various colours. At the rehearsal the players were told to keep certain colours in their minds which were represented by different movements.[10] Being a highly disciplined force they obediently carried out their instructions. But after the rehearsal had been going on for some time and the performers were becoming somewhat tired and thirsty, one wind player feelingly asked his next-door neighbour, "When are we coming to 'Black and White'?"

---

10   This is a clear reference to Bliss's *Colour Symphony*, which received its first performance at the 1922 Gloucester Three Choirs Festival under the composer's direction. Elgar considered the work to be 'disconcertingly modern'. See above, p.87, fn.11.

Of pupils I have had many and of varying ability, amongst them such contrasts as the serious-minded Herbert Howells and the light-hearted Ivor Novello.[11] Then there are the 'would-be' musicians – the private pupils – many are the stories I could relate of their curious sayings and doings. At one time a friend of mine held a living near Gloucester, and eked out his small stipend by coaching private pupils. What a life that poor man must have led! He came to me one day and told me that he could only keep one of the boys on the condition that I took him as a piano pupil. He intimated that the youth was very backward in school work, but well advanced in music. Wishing to do the parson a good turn I consented – perhaps foolishly – without seeing the boy or hearing him play. The day arrived for his first lesson. He brought some very elementary music, and at once seated himself at the piano to display the great gifts his parents imagined he possessed. It did not take me long to discover that his knowledge of music was nil. The piece he had chosen to perform was in the key of C, and was marked four crotchets in a bar. I pointed out to him that he should remember to give the full value to all the notes, adding that a dotted minim should be held down for three beats. When he came to the next dotted minim I asked him how long he should hold it down. He promptly replied "three *weeks!*" I told him to put on his 'thinking-cap'. He solemnly rose from the piano seat, and, looking round my study, said, "I think I must have left it in the hall, Sir!"

Another youth about nineteen years of age, who was with the same tutor, wished to learn singing. He had not a bad voice and possessed a fairly good ear, so I decided to try and teach him one or two songs. I told him to get Schumann's *Two Grenadiers*,[12] which he did, but he brought it in the wrong key and so I had to transpose it. I told him that he must bring the song in the correct key the next week. When he arrived he brought the same copy, and I had to transpose it again. Then I asked him how he had managed with his accompanist when practising the song. His reply was rather staggering. He said,

---

11 Again, one must regret the absence of Ivor Gurney's name (see also above, p.93, fn.8). Brewer might also have mentioned Herbert Sumsion, who was his articled pupil from 1914 to 1917, and who, in accordance with Brewer's wishes, succeeded him at Gloucester. See Boden, pp.172–3.
12 *Die Beiden Grenadiere* (Op.49, No.1).

"Well, you see, Sir, it is like this, my tutor's wife is not so musical as you are, and she can't transpose; so she plays it in the key it's written in, and I sing it a note lower!" Needless to say these two musical prodigies did not run their full course. I do not know what happened to them, but I do know that my friend, the parson, had a serious breakdown, and was ordered a complete rest.

The third case was of a lady who wrote me a letter saying, "A line to say my daughter has been singing for some time past, and now I want her finished off. Could you undertake this?" A subtle question this. On the face of it the expression – "undertake" and "finished off" – seem to be singularly significant. But why should I be invited to do the deed? All this happened, too, before I became High Sheriff.

– 15 –

1913–22

There were many unforgettable things in connection with the
1913 Festival at Gloucester. Chief among these was the visit of
Camille Saint-Saëns. The great French composer not only produced
a new oratorio, but also appeared as solo pianist at the secular
concert. This was the only occasion on which Saint-Saëns had had
a work produced at an English festival. He originally called the
work *Moses in Egypt*, but altered the title to *The Promised Land*.
Unfortunately it did not come up to expectations. Most people
agreed that it would have been better had he not succumbed to
the temptation to revive an enthusiasm which he felt a quarter of
a century before for the subject. Had he carried out his idea then,
there is no doubt whatever that his work would have been of wider
and deeper interest.[1] Orchestra, soloists and chorus vied with each
other in giving of their best to the composer, who conducted his
work, and the result was an admirable performance. Recognized as
the greatest exponent of Mozart's music Saint-Saëns was invited to
play that composer's Pianoforte Concerto in B flat.[2] His deft execution
and the charm of his touch and phrasing carried the audience away,
and it was a real tribute of enthusiasm which the aged composer
won from his hearers. In response to the tremendous applause he
played his *Mignonne Valse*. When a man is verging on eighty years
of age one regards his appearance as concert soloist at an important
festival as a phenomenon.[3]

Before leaving Gloucester he sent me the following letter:

---

1   For a contemporary appraisal see Herbert Thompson, 'New Oratorio by Dr Saint-
Saëns: "The Promised Land", *Musical Times*, 54 (1913), pp.508–12. Herman Klein,
who supplied the text for the oratorio, provides an account of the work's reception
in 'Camille Saint-Saëns 1835–1921: Saint-Saëns as I Knew Him', *Musical Times*,
63 (1922), pp.90–93.
2   No.27 (K.595).
3   Saint-Saëns was a virtuoso pianist, as his surviving piano rolls attest.

11 Sept. 1913

(Translation)
Dear Dr Brewer
    Would you please give my warm thanks to your fine orchestra and excellent choir for the able and sympathetic rendering they gave of my work "The Promised Land." It was a great pleasure to me to hear it for the first time under such wonderful conditions.

Your very devoted colleague
C. Saint-Saëns

Another feature of this Festival was the singing of Madame Ackté,[4] who came from Finland to take part in Verdi's *Requiem* and to produce a new work, *Luonnotar*[5] – a tone poem, which Sibelius had specially written for her. At the rehearsal she caused much resentment by the way she insisted on the withdrawal of the audience, which consisted chiefly of the members of the chorus who do not sing at the secular concert, and who were naturally anxious to hear the Finnish star. Her action was fully justified, for the music that she sang required so perfect an understanding between orchestra and singer that a detailed rehearsal was more than necessary. In fact parts of the score of *Luonnotar* were "still in his head" a fortnight before the Festival, so the composer said. The orchestral parts were hastily copied out and full of errors.[6] However, the difficulties were surmounted, and the composition with all its atmospheric and original effect made a great impression.

Few singers could express its extraordinary wistfulness as Madame Ackté did. Still more sensational was her singing of the closing scene from Strauss's *Salome*. Never in living memory had such singing in such music been heard at a Three Choirs Festival. It was electrifying, and the audience was worked up to a wild state of enthusiasm.

---

4   Aino Ackté (1876–1944), Finnish soprano.
5   i.e. 'Daughter of Nature'. Brewer consistently misspells the work *Luonotar*.
6   Sibelius's diary entry for 5 September 1913 – two days after rehearsing the work with the soloist (who had received it only a few days earlier) – records his irritation at the haste under which he was required to compose: "She sang well, but how far I am from perfection when I have to hurry my work, and when time cannot improve the craftsmanship!"

After the Festival Sibelius wrote:

Finland
19 September 1913

(Translation)
My dear Doctor
How can I thank you for the excellent performance of
my work!
When I wrote my last short letter I was unhappy about
part of Luonnotar, which still had to be revised; therefore
it was very wrong of ... to send it off.
May I trouble you to write to Mr. Wood[7] and ask him
kindly to send "Luonnotar" to me. I unfortunately do not
know his address.
I congratulate you on your great success.
With kindest regards

Your truly grateful
Jean Sibelius

Other works included in the scheme were Elgar's *Dream of
Gerontius* and his Symphony in E flat (No.2), and Bach's *Passion*.[8]
Stanford's unaccompanied motet, *Ye Holy Angels Bright*, had a first
hearing, and gave the chorus an opportunity of proving their real
value. The secular concert included a novelty from W. H. Reed's pen,
Will of the Wisp, and my Ballad, *Sir Patrick Spens*. After the first
day of the Festival I was greatly amused to read on a placard in huge
print – 'Gloucester Festival Sensation Elijah Hustled'. I lost no time
in purchasing the paper, wondering whether the Prophet had made
a re-appearance! But I was to discover that I had given a daring
interpretation of Mendelssohn's work and created a great sensation
by ending at least fifteen minutes before the scheduled time. That
was all! Poor conductor!
To solve the mystery I should explain that the time announced
for the luncheon interval had been copied from the programme of
the previous Festival, on which occasion *Elijah* had been preceded

7   Sir Henry Wood (1869–1944).
8   The *St Matthew Passion*. The first performance of Bach's *St John Passion* at a
Three Choirs Festival was at Worcester in 1929.

by Sullivan's *In Memoriam* Overture in memory of King Edward VII. On the occasion in question the overture was not played, and so the duration of the programme was lessened by about the same number of minutes as I was supposed to have gained in the first part of *Elijah*. In reviewing the week's performances a London critic says: "I cannot help thinking that this year's meeting will come to be regarded in musical history as the Festival of the Gloucester Choir." To this fact the following letter from Parry also bears testimony, and it was probably the last letter he wrote in connection with the Three Choirs:

Sep. 12, 1913

My dear Brewer

How those dear chorus people did sing to-day, bless them! I never enjoyed anything more than feeling they were entirely giving themselves with all their hearts to respond to every point the conductor gave them. And after all the work they have gone through it shews a splendid loyalty to you and to the Festival and to all those whose works they have been interpreting. Of course we never had a finer chorus nor a more intelligent one or a more devoted one. And also of course our old friends of the band are as finely musical as technically efficient, and such good willing hearty friends. When one thinks of the huge undertakings of ultra modern music which they willingly and surely face, and how they compare with what was required of them a quarter of a century ago it makes one not only content with the musical growth of the country but enthusiastically confident of our constant advance in capacity and understanding.

And your own huge task! I do think that if people could realize the infinite variety of qualifications it requires they would feel that our western country ought to recognize you as one of the most able and distinguished of its sons.

Yours ever most sincerely
C. Hubert H. Parry

Nobody could foresee at the close of this Festival what was to happen before the next Meeting took place, and what changes there would be in the personnel of these ancient Festivals. Before the outbreak of war the following year all preparations had been made for the Worcester Meeting. The chorus had been rehearsing for months, soloists and orchestra had been engaged, when suddenly the terrible catastrophe fell on us and caused an upheaval of the whole musical world. Less than a month before the Festival the Stewards at Worcester decided that it was impossible to carry their Music Meeting through, and so their Festival was indefinitely postponed.

Many members of the orchestra and chorus who had long been associated with the Three Choirs made the great sacrifice, and before we met again death had robbed these historic Music Meetings of three of their greatest supporters – Parry, Lloyd and Sinclair. The last named I have already referred to in a previous chapter.[9] To Parry, who died early in 1918, the Three Choirs Festivals, and Gloucester in particular, owe a great debt of gratitude. The enlarging of the Shire Hall will be a lasting memorial to his great generosity. Whilst speaking of his large-heartedness I should like to relate an incident which probably few know, and which bears testimony to that side of his nature. A student at the Royal College of Music came to Parry one day to ask his help and criticism of a setting of *The Pied Piper of Hamelin*. Parry, who had already set the poem to music, put his own composition away in a drawer, and threw himself whole-heartedly into the student's work. Whether that work was ever published I cannot say, but eventually Parry's setting saw daylight and is now, I suppose, one of the most popular of his works.

Of his great creative talent it is needless to speak. Posterity will decide the exact position he should occupy amongst the world's composers. His vocal writing was always gratefully planned, and he did not treat the voice as an orchestral instrument as so many modern composers do. He had not a great orchestral sense, and his oratorios suffer in consequence. For instance – much of the fine dramatic choral writing of *Job* is marred by ineffective orchestra-tion. Parry's death may be said to have coincided with the close of the oratorio in its original form of set numbers. Whether that form is permanently dead time alone will prove.

Lloyd's death on his seventieth birthday in October, 1919, came as a great blow to me. From the beginning of our acquaintance a bond

9   See Chapter 2.

of affection sprang up between us, and our friendship remained firm and intimate until the end of his life; in fact, I doubt if anyone knew him better than I did. We shared our joys and sorrows during the long period of forty-three years, and his death caused a gap in my life which it is impossible to fill. He was the most unselfish and generous of men, with an intensely keen sense of duty, and he consistently lived up to the very high ideals he had of life. Although very young at the time, I well remember the consternation in the musical world caused by the appointment of the young Oxford musician to succeed as organist of Gloucester Cathedral one of the greatest musical geniuses of the last century, Dr S. S. Wesley. But the choice was soon justified, and the wholehearted way in which he threw himself into the musical life of the city immediately met with excellent results. His great gifts as an extempore player had already been appreciated by Wesley, and he had few equals in this difficult branch of his art. His performances never lacked form and design. As a writer of English church music he proved himself a worthy successor to the great English composers. His compositions were always marked by refinement and excellent workmanship, and his loss as a composer of church music, madrigals and motets is great. His motet, *The righteous live for evermore*, composed for the Gloucester Festival in 1901, will be a lasting monument to his genius.

His was an extremely highly strung, nervous temperament, and illustrative of this I remember an occasion on which he was conducting in the nave of Gloucester Cathedral, and his assistant at the organ failed to follow his beat. Throwing down his baton, Lloyd rushed up into the organ-loft and flung aside the assistant, who came in audible contact with the floor, and played himself. I recollect Lloyd telling me of a rehearsal of a well-known Society in London which he had been asked to conduct, and how he had pulled up the basses for faulty singing. He thought no more about it, but at the end of the rehearsal one of the basses went up to him and asked him what he meant by pulling them up. He went on to say that they didn't go there to have their mistakes pointed out, but to enjoy themselves!

Lloyd was a man of great versatility, being not only a highly gifted musician, a scholar of no mean worth, and an accomplished linguist, but also a keen participator in outdoor pastimes. This fact probably accounted for his perpetual youth. As a young man he was an energetic mountaineer and skater, and in later years he became an enthusiastic golfer.

The last service Lloyd played was on Sunday, October 12th, 1919. He died the following Thursday. During the previous week he had been able to prepare the music for that day, including the Psalms for the 12th morning. To his horror on the Sunday morning the Sub-Dean of the Chapel Royal gave out the Psalm for the *13th* morning. Lloyd saw immediately what was likely to happen – the men would probably sing the Psalm given out and the boys the one which they had prepared. To avert a catastrophe he rose from his seat and said, "The 12th morning Psalms, *not* the 13th," and so saved the situation. He was ever alert and prepared for any emergency.

Lloyd often told me that the happiest years of his life were spent at Gloucester. That being so, what more appropriate place than the Cathedral in which to erect a memorial? After consulting the Dean and Chapter, who readily gave their consent to the suggestion, it was decided to place a window to his memory in the 'musicians' corner' in the Lady Chapel, facing that of his predecessor, S. S. Wesley. The necessary amount for the window was raised by giving organ recitals and collecting subscriptions. The subscriptions came in so well that I decided not only to place a window in the cathedral but also to found a fund for a scholarship for ex-cathedral choristers who intended adopting music as a profession – an idea which would certainly have appealed to Lloyd himself. The window was unveiled on Tuesday, February 7th, 1922, by his lifelong friend, Sir Henry Hadow, Vice-Chancellor of Sheffield University. The scholarship idea gave such general satisfaction and so appealed to the organizers of the Parry memorial that they decided to devote the remainder of the money, after paying for the tablet in the Cathedral, to founding a 'Parry Scholarship' at Gloucester on the same lines. And so the memory of both Gloucestershire musicians will be kept fresh in the minds of young musicians for generations to come.[10]

---

10   Lloyd was a high-ranking Freemason, and was appointed Grand Organist in 1917. Amongst other Three Choirs organists to have held this appointment were G. R. Sinclair (1902) and Sir Percy Hull (1922). Other friends and associates of Brewer who are mentioned in his *Memories* and who served as Grand Organist include Dr Henry Davan Wetton (1903) and the Bristol Cathedral organist Hubert Hunt (1919). Brewer himself does not appear to have been a Freemason.

All through the period of the war the activities of the Choral and Orchestral Societies were maintained, and the concerts afforded welcome relaxation to many upon whom war work inflicted a great strain. The profits were devoted to war charities.

It was during this period – the summer of 1915 – that I had rather an amusing experience in Cornwall. I had motored to Mullion to stay with my friend, Samuel Aitken, whose name was familiar to many musicians of the past generation as the first secretary of the Associated Board of the Royal Academy of Music and the Royal College of Music,[11] and an amateur musician with gifts of no ordinary order. Mr Aitken's bungalow was right on the cliff overlooking the wild, rugged Cornish coast, which gets the full force of the Atlantic at this particular spot. Arriving there in the evening I was strolling on the cliff before dinner and sitting down for a few minutes to enjoy the glorious scenery [when] a stranger came and sat beside me. He at once entered into conversation, and after discussing the weather and other topics of the moment he inquired whether I had been in that part of England before; how long I intended to remain; what did I think of the German submarines; how long was it since I had been in Germany; did I think England would be beaten; in what regiment had I been? All these questions were rolled out one after the other without giving me an opportunity of replying, and I noticed that, as each question was put, the little man raised his voice and became more agitated, and beads of perspiration stood out on his forehead. When he did stop to take breath I told him that I had only arrived there that evening on a visit to Mr Aitken. On hearing Mr Aitken's name he heaved a sigh of relief, and taking his handkerchief from his pocket and mopping his forehead, he said, "Then you are the gentleman who arrived in a car this evening?" On my replying in the affirmative he exclaimed, "Thank God! We all thought you were a German spy!"

We became fast friends after that, and many a yarn he spun me of smugglers and what-not. He had a portion of the cliff to patrol every day, and I always knew where to find my little friend after that amusing episode. It was in a neighbouring village to Mullion that there lived a certain farm labourer who caused considerable anxiety

---

11   Now the Associated Board of the Royal Schools of Music. Little is known about
     Aitken, though he is believed to have been a friend of Sir Arthur Sullivan.

to his relatives, not to mention the local vicar, by his ever-consuming thirst. Everything possible was done to get this man to sign the pledge, but all efforts were unavailing. However, at a subsequent temperance gathering in the village, to everyone's astonishment, "Jarge" was seen to be occupying a prominent seat. The next day the vicar, meeting him in the road and thinking that he had at last perceived the folly of his ways, remarked how pleased he had been to see him at the meeting on the previous evening. "Oh," mused Jarge, scratching his head, "that's w'er' I wer', wer' I?"

The return journey to Gloucester was a never-to-be-forgotten drive. Before leaving Mullion at 8 a.m. my friends said that if I were anything of a sport I should go through in the day and not take two days over the journey, as I did when I was travelling *to* Mullion. The distance was 237 miles, the car an eight-horse-power two-seater Swift with a twin-cylinder engine. There were four of us – my wife and two children[12] besides myself – in the car, and all our luggage on the back; so that we were a heavy load for a car of that size and power with the Cornish and Devonshire hills in front of us. We got as far as Exeter with little trouble, but when we reached the centre of the town, where the street is very narrow, the car suddenly stopped and held up all the traffic. With the help of the police and good-natured citizens we were pushed into a side street where the trouble was put right, and we started again on our journey. Up to that time we had only had half an hour's break for lunch, and that was the only meal we had during the journey, our pangs of hunger being appeased by eating bananas as we drove along. As we passed through each town I thought of the inconvenience of unpacking for the night and pressed on.

One unfortunate incident happened on the way. A sheep, which was being chased by a dog, charged into the car and committed

---

12 Bernard/Godfrey Noel (b.1901) and Eileen Mary (b.1905); the Brewers' first son – Charles Herbert (b.1895) – would have been about twenty years old by this time. The official entry in the Gloucester Registration book records that their second son was originally registered as Bernard Noel, but there is a note to the effect that he was baptised as *Godfrey* Noel. Presumably when the details were sent to the General Register Office the forename Godfrey was adopted as being the more recent choice. Godfrey Brewer was a career naval officer, and commanded HMS Pelican during the Second World War, during which he was awarded the DSO. His brother Charles had been awarded the MC in the First World War.

suicide. Fortunately for me the owner agreed that it was not my fault – a most unusual experience for a motorist – and I was able to continue my journey. As soon as we left Bristol we ran into waves of fog, and what with the fog and my small daughter asleep on my arm I found driving somewhat difficult. But all's well that ends well, and we drove into Gloucester the same night at 12 p.m. I felt proud of the achievement until one day, when relating my experience to Filson Young,[13] he told me of his journey of 1,000 miles through France and Italy without a break. Since then I have hesitated to tell of my drive of 237 miles, though it is only fair to say that Filson Young's car was not a twin-cylinder eight-horse-power Swift.[14]

---

13   Filson Young (1876–1938), author.
14   Brewer was an enthusiastic motorist, citing 'motoring' as his sole recreation in his entry in *Who's Who*.

– 16 –

Miscellaneous reminiscences

Some years ago Dame Clara Butt expressed a wish to produce one of my songs.[1] Several months passed and I had not written anything that I considered suitable for her, when one night, as I was locking up the house and going to bed, I happened to glance at a lyric which Fred E. Weatherly[2] had sent me; and immediately a tune wedded itself to the words, and within half an hour I had written what proved to be the most popular song I have ever composed – *The Fairy Pipers*. Dame Clara sang it on her world tour in 1913–14, and, in an interview on her return, mentioned that the world-favourite was *The Fairy Pipers*.

In connection with this song a rather amusing play upon words was perpetrated by a provincial paper after it had been sung at a concert in Bath. The report ran thus:

> "The Fairy Pipers" was sung last night at the "Pump" Rooms. It was written for a "Butt" by a composer named "Brewer" and published by a "Boozy" firm. On this occasion it was sung by Madame "Drinkwater" and accompanied by Mr "Tapp." The audience was "intoxicated" with delight long before the last "bar" closed!

Whilst speaking of songs the following letter from Sir Arthur Quiller-Couch is an example of the kindly assistance sometimes extended by authors to composers:[3]

---

1 Dame Clara Butt (1872–1936) was a noted contralto who specialised in concert and recital work.
2 Frederic Edward Weatherly (1848–1929), lawyer, author and lyricist. His lyrics include those of the popular songs *Danny Boy* and *Roses of Picardy*.
3 The Cornish author (1863–1944), who published under the pseudonym 'Q'. It is difficult to know whether Brewer's reference to the 'kindly assistance' extended to him by Quiller-Couch is intended to be taken seriously, or whether it is merely a 'tongue-in-cheek' comment on its over-prescriptiveness.

The Haven
Fowey, Cornwall
March 4th, 1912

My dear Sir

Many thanks for letting me see a proof of the song, which I am returning. It is full of character and I like it very much: but I hope you won't mind a small criticism or two offered very diffidently.

I don't think – if it may be said – that there's enough emphasis, in the setting, to mark the *"internal rhymes"* which were in fact the experiment upon which I wrote the verses.

> To Bodmin town from *Scorrier*
> Like a *warrior* all ablaze
> With knapsack, pouch and *bagginet*
> In a *wagginet* drawn by bays

and so on.

In writing with a drum and fife in my mind, I "sort of heard" the side-drum giving a rattle on these rhymes – or a rattle on the first and an echoing rattle on the second (the "internal" rhyme) to mark it; and I would (diffidently again, let it be repeated) suggest that – this should be marked in the air by a sharp triplet, even if the sharp rattle of a drum cannot be achieved in the accompaniment. I wouldn't mention this if I didn't like your setting so very much that I feel it worth while to be extremely frank.

> Form up, my sons of Waterloo
> (rub-a-dub)
> For a mortal who can't behave
> (rub-a-dub)

That really, is the *clue* of the metrical intention of the verses.

(2) A minor criticism. I don't care for the rallentando on "to the grave." This follows in a way on the other criticism. I should go slow and solemn on

> To bring my hairs in sorrow down
> With a —

and then introduce the unexpected with

rataplan to the grave
(rub-a-dub)

very smart and military. That would give, I think, the right absurd touch.

I ought to tell you that, as published in the Cornish Magazine, each verse had a chorus. This is probably too late for you now, unless you think it worth while to popularize the thing. The chorus is –

One and all,
Little men and tall,
With a thirty-nine average chest;
And there isn't a corps
That could give "what for"
To the Duke-of-Cornwall's-best!

"One and all" motto of the County and of the Duke of Cornwall's Light Infantry.

Last line to be sung in careful staccato, rall.

In last verse

And there *isn't* a corps
That *can* give "what for"

Forgive all this. I *do* like the setting very much. That's really the reason why I so much want to like it better.

Yours very truly
Arthur Quiller-Couch

Dr A. Herbert Brewer

I wonder if any other composer has found his name a hindrance to the performance of his music. Some time ago a cathedral organist told me that his Bishop, who was a rabid teetotaller, objected to the inclusion of 'Brewer in E flat' in the service scheme when he had to preach! I have never heard of such an objection before, though I have met dignitaries of the church who complained of the *length* of anthems. A Canon of a northern cathedral, for instance, kept a Novello's catalogue in his stall, and when the anthem was given out he referred to the price list. If it was marked twopence he stood up, but if it was marked fourpence he sat down. Time was when members of the Cathedral Chapter would sometimes criticize the choice of music – as a rule the greatest objectors knowing least about it – but times have changed, and my experience during a long period is that Deans and Chapters now give every encouragement and support to their 'chief musician'.

I cannot refrain from quoting a letter which I received from one who set himself up as an authority in music in my very early days of cathedral life. He says:

> I requested the Precentor never again during my 'resi-
> dence' to put up J— in G, after hearing its loathsome and
> meaningless crudities a few weeks ago. My request has
> evidently slipped his memory. I must therefore request you
> to step into his place and substitute something that one
> can listen to without disgust next Sunday. J— and W—
> I have resolved never again to listen to, and shall absent
> myself from Cathedral whenever they are on the bill: this
> I cannot do while in 'residence.'

I do not know what the modern musician would think of the 'loathsome and meaningless crudities' referred to, considering that that particular style of music is now condemned as old-fashioned! Another official strongly objected to S— in A, and, after the service one day, harangued the choristers on this composer's music, and said that if this service was ever sung again he would walk out. Quite unconscious of what had taken place, I selected the same service for the following day (Sunday), as it had gone so well and I had been unable to prepare the music which had been put down for performance. When this dear old gentleman discovered what was going to be sung he instructed the verger at the close of the First Lesson to 'poker' him out of the choir into the vestry. This the verger accordingly did; but not knowing the reason for this procedure, after the Second Lesson, he 'pokered' him back to his stall so that, in spite of his precautions, the unfortunate official had to stand and listen to the *Nunc Dimittis* of S— in A! However, he survived, and, as I say, times have changed, and the ears of the most unmusical have been trained and accustomed to more modern harmonies than in the days about which I write.

Every cathedral organist has had experience of requests for performances of compositions by amateur composers, not infre-quently of the fair sex. I have a vivid memory of one lady (whose husband occupied a very high position in the Church) who spent much time in writing music to well-known hymns, such as the Easter hymn – *Jesus Christ is risen today*. These she wanted sung at the services in the Cathedral, but I had to point out to her, as gently as I could, how impossible it was to do this, as the congregation was so accustomed to the tunes which were wedded to the words. She then sent me a setting of a less well-known hymn, and, unfortunately, at the particular request of one of the Canons, I allowed it to be sung. I say 'unfortunately' with intention because, after its performance, there was a constant flow of hymn tunes, which were sent with a plea that they should be sung on the following Sunday. These requests came from members of the Chapter as well as from the lady herself. I decided that steps must be taken to damp the ardour of this prolific composer, and I told her that she would never write a better tune than the first one. "Oh, won't I?" she said. "I will go on till I do."

She promptly proceeded to carry out her threat. The amount of MS. paper she used was prodigious. I did not know how to put an end to it, and at last suggested that her thoughts should be turned to other forms of music. It happened to be at the time that the Coronation of King Edward VII was postponed on account of his illness.[4] This calamity inspired her to write an anthem, the title of which, *The King was Sick*, will ever remain in my memory. In the setting she dwelt on the third word an unnecessary length of time with the following result – "The King *was* – sick" – which made it all the more ludicrous. I do not remember the source of the words, but I do remember that those members of the Chapter who had so strongly advocated the singing of her hymn tunes felt that this was the last straw, and she was told that the title of the work made the performance of it impossible. This was, I believe, her last inspiration as a composer.

During the war a newspaper controversy took place about the performance of German music and the singing of German hymn tunes in our churches, one parson having gone so far as to forbid the playing of the *Dead March in Saul* on account of its German origin; though the English, as a nation, showed little desire to

---

4   Edward VII succeeded to the throne on Queen Victoria's death in 1901. The Coronation was originally set for 26 June 1902, on which date the King was hospitalized for an emergency appendectomy. The Coronation eventually took place on 9 August 1902.

import the bitterness of war into their musical appreciation. I wonder if churchgoers realize how many of their favourite hymns are of German extraction.

We have a long and honourable list of English hymns with German tunes which have identified themselves with the deepest and most solemn thoughts of the English, and we should be the poorer if they were excluded from our public worship. A process of selection has been going on for two centuries, and, probably, the best collection has been made in England. Sir Walter Parratt laid his finger upon a musical fact of considerable import when he said that the last great German composer died in the nineties. Wagner, who is not altogether free from degenerate tendencies himself, is said to have viewed with apprehension the rapidly increasing tendency amongst his fellow countrymen to consecrate every talent they had on war and war preparation, and that this had a degenerating effect on art and music. In support of this, let me instance a contrast which came in my own course of work. Only a short time ago I gave two performances of the inspired and beautiful *German Requiem* by Brahms, and one could not help contrasting it with the closing Scene from *Salome* by Strauss, which I conducted at the Three Choirs Festival in 1922, with its ear-splitting, nerve-racking, hideous, discordant noises.[5]

One of the many striking developments of the war has been a great outpouring of literary ability among the young men who faced the actualities of warfare, not in the love of war for war's own sake, of which Wagner spoke, but who went into war because they loved freedom and justice more than life.

It is a little early in the day to say whether there will be a similar renaissance of musical ability. There are many musicians of great promise in England. Some of these in the past, I am afraid, have succumbed not infrequently to the miasmatic influence of the baser kind of modern German musicians. But I do not doubt that they will now rise to a far higher conception of what has been done by their own countrymen in the past – men like Purcell, Byrd, Gibbons and others – who have left us a goodly heritage of church music, and

---

5   In view of Brewer's dislike of *Salome* it is rather surprising that he agreed to conduct it.

that they will carry on this glorious tradition. In order to improve congregational singing and the popular taste in hymns, a movement has been inaugurated in Gloucestershire through the initiative, and under the guidance, of Sir Henry Hadow, to hold hymn festivals in various parts of the county; and it is hoped that this venture will spread and take root throughout the land.

The form of procedure is to select a number of good hymns for performance at the festival, and these are rehearsed by separate congregations, under the instruction of their organist or vicar, at practices usually held after Sunday evening service. After a period of rehearsal the congregations meet together at the largest and most central church of the district; the services of a capable conductor are requisitioned, who rehearses and gives advice and instruction to the combined congregations. The Festival then takes place, and those who have hitherto been in the habit of joining feebly and timorously in the hymns, attack with precision, and sing lustily and heartily; and the effect produced is both thrilling and inspiring.

It is a strange trait in human nature that the majority of people are not troubled with sensitive consciences when a voluntary contribution towards the expenses of a musical service is asked of them. They will not hesitate to pay for a seat at a concert – or any other form of entertainment for which a fixed charge is made; but when a performance takes place in a church or cathedral it does not seem to occur to the average listener that he is under a moral obligation to place in the plate a coin, the value of which is commensurate with the enjoyment he derives therefrom. In fact with the majority of people it would seem that the smaller the coin they can contrive to put in the plate the better pleased they are.

The authorities at Westminster, after a musical service in the Abbey, drew attention to this reluctance of the general public to contribute to the collections in a manner proportionate to the enthusiasm they displayed in seeking admission on these occasions. I am convinced that this apparent meanness is due in a great measure to thoughtlessness. If the promoters of musical services would take the congregation into their confidence and tell them the exact sum required they would get a generous response. People are apt to expect so much for nothing, often imagining cathedral staffs to be so well paid and capitular bodies so rich that such bodies themselves can afford to bear the expenses of these special services.

In support of my theory I would instance the collections which are made at the close of the performances at the Three Choirs Festivals. The people know that their offerings are to be given to the widows and orphans of the clergy of the three dioceses. Although the price of tickets at the last one held at Gloucester[6] ranged from seventeen and six downwards, no less a sum than £740 6s. 4d. was collected at the doors for the charity.

In connection with offertories I can relate a pretty little story of a small child who came to one of my organ recitals with her mother. When the time came for the collection, she expressed a wish to her mother to put something in the bag. In due course the collector appeared before her and, looking up into his face as she dropped the coin into the bag, she said, "That's for the organ man." She had a definite object for her donation!

---

6   In 1922.

− 17 −

Organ recitals for children

In the autumn of 1918 the Dean and Chapter of Manchester did me the honour of offering me the position of organist at the Cathedral, which had become vacant through the appointment of S. H. Nicholson[1] to Westminster Abbey. When the Gloucester authorities heard of the proposal they offered me several inducements to remain in Gloucester. One was the augmenting of the Cathedral choir by four extra men for the Sunday services. They also sanctioned my scheme for the re-building of the organ, and gave me such sympathetic support in every way that I decided not to sever my connection with Gloucester and declined the invitation to go to the North.[2]

I thereupon devoted my energies to collecting the necessary funds for the re-building of the organ, for which I had undertaken to be responsible. My task was soon unexpectedly to be made easy for me by the great generosity of Sir James and Lady Horlick,[3] who undertook to defray the cost of reconstruction in memory of their son, Major Gerald Horlick, who died on active service.[4] At the same time the opportunity was taken to lower the pitch of the organ, which had long been a source of trouble at Festival times.

---

1   Sir Sydney Nicholson (1875–1947) was organist of Westminster Abbey from 1919 to 1928. He took early retirement in order to establish the School of English Church Music (later the Royal School of Church Music) at Chislehurst, Kent.

2   It is surprising that Brewer should have regarded a move from Gloucester to Manchester as a promotion. Interestingly Sir Sydney Nicholson, who had accepted the appointment as organist at Canterbury Cathedral in 1908, withdrew his acceptance in order to accept the Manchester vacancy. The Ely Cathedral organist Archibald Wilson (1869–1950) was eventually appointed to replace Nicholson at Manchester. See Shaw, *The Succession of Organists*, p.50.

3   Sir James Horlick (1844–1921) was created 1st Baronet in 1914. A plaque recording the 1920 reconstruction and enlargement of the organ can be seen at the entrance to the organ-loft.

4   Major Gerald Nolekin Horlick of the Royal Gloucestershire Hussars died on 5 July 1918. The family fortune derived from the patented malted milk products of the same name.

The work was entrusted to Messrs. Harrison of Durham with such satisfactory results that no organist could wish for a more beautiful instrument on which to perform. During the alterations an amusing experience happened to me when I was discussing with Mr Arthur Harrison in the nave the most suitable place for the 32-foot pipes. Two young men, accompanied by three or four young ladies, approached us, and one of the men asked me if I could tell him where a verger could be found who would take them round the Cathedral. I thought that perhaps he knew me by sight, and that that was his reason for asking me the question. I soon found a verger who would be disengaged in a few minutes, and on returning to the party the young man said to me, "I see the organ is under repair," and he went on to say, "I knew Dr Brewer, who used to be organist here, very well before he died." A cold, clammy feeling came over me, and I found that I was pinching myself to see if I was really alive. When I recovered my breath I ventured to ask the young man if he wasn't thinking of either Dr Lloyd or Dr Sinclair, who were both dead. "No," he replied emphatically, "I knew them, but it was Dr Brewer who was my particular friend." I was not conscious of ever having seen the man before. At that moment the verger appeared, and so cut short the conversation. When they had gone Mr Harrison expressed surprise at my not undeceiving the young man, but I explained to him that I did not wish to be unkind and give him away in front of his lady friends. The organ was completed, and the dedication service took place on November 19th, 1920.

The idea of giving organ recitals to the elementary schoolchildren of Gloucester had occurred to me some time previously, and as soon as the organ was finished I proceeded to carry it out. The lines upon which I conceived them are so simple that they could be carried on equally well in the smallest village church as in a cathedral. There is no expense attached to them, and *no* collection. At the beginning of the week a typed programme is sent out to the schools which are to attend, and the teachers read it aloud to the children, who write it in their notebooks and, in addition, memorize the hymn. The intention is to give the children the opportunity to become acquainted with the works of the great masters, and the most simple and tuneful pieces are given to begin with. In time it is hoped that the children will be able to appreciate more elaborate music. It will be seen by the notes on the composers that only the barest facts are given, so as to

Sir Herbert Brewer at the organ console of Gloucester Cathedral, following its reconstruction in 1920.

Photograph originally published in *The Times*. *Copyright holder untraced.*

enable the children to remember a little about each one, and point is made of local connections.

The recitals do not last more than three-quarters of an hour. The same programme is played each week until all the children between the ages of ten and fourteen have attended in turn. Marshalled by their teachers, and armed with pencil and paper for the purpose of making notes, they arrive at the cathedral with military punctuality and precision, and are received and directed to their seats by the secretary to the City Educational Committee and myself. We begin with the Lord's Prayer. Then I tell the children in simple words exactly what they are going to hear, and how to listen to it. For one of the series the hymn selected was *O God, our help in ages past* to the tune 'St Anne'. I explained to them that, after the singing of the hymn, I should play the Fugue which Bach had written on that tune. I then defined a fugue, and told them to notice and write down every time the subject recurred.

I was told afterwards that it was astonishing to observe the extreme attention of the children and the rapidity with which they used their pencils, even in the middle movement and finale, where the subject turns up unexpectedly in various rhythmic forms, those children in doubt obviously consulting each other on the subject. If boys and girls of tender age can thus be taught and given an insight into the real meaning of the higher branches of musical art, there seems to be a vast future for musical missionaries.

At the close of the first series I received a number of letters from these small people saying how greatly they had appreciated the recitals, and expressing the hope that they would be continued. Needless to say I valued very highly these spontaneous expressions of gratitude. After the recitals the children write essays on what they have seen as well as heard, some of them illustrating these with sketches of the Cathedral, and many of the efforts of these young commentators are extremely interesting, and display talent of no mean order, some being of very high merit indeed. So impressed was I with their work that I decided to give prizes for the best essays, and these they receive at the annual prize-giving. The local educational authorities have given their wholehearted support to the movement, and the recitals are recognized as part of the afternoon curriculum of the children's schoolwork.

Mr H. A. L. Fisher, Minister of Education at the time of their inauguration, expressed his approval and support of the recitals in the following letter:[5]

Board of Education
Whitehall, London, S.W.I
7th March, 1921

Dear Sir

    I have been interested to learn of this new enterprise in Gloucester of giving organ recitals for school children, and I am grateful to those connected with the Cathedral who have helped on the movement. There can be no reason why children, even so young as those in our elementary schools, should not come to enjoy good music if they can be made sufficiently familiar with it. A single hearing has, I suppose, very little educative value. The important point seems to me that the same children should have an opportunity of repeatedly hearing suitable music by the great composers. You may be interested to know that a special series of orchestral concerts have been given as part of a scheme of music "appreciation" in several towns. I can think of Newcastle, Bradford, Nottingham, and Oxford under Sir Hugh Allen. I am anxious that musical societies should help in this way, and find an outlet for their enthusiasm in the education of children in musical appreciation.

Yours very truly
H. A. L. Fisher

Apart from any benefit the children may derive from the music, the very fact of spending a short time in a building so imposing and of such architectural beauty as Gloucester Cathedral must have an uplifting and refining effect. That this is the case in many instances is proved by their recorded impressions.

---

5   Herbert Albert Laurens Fisher OM (1865–1940), the distinguished historian, educator and Liberal politician, served in Lloyd George's coalition government from 1916 to 1922. He was Warden of New College, Oxford from 1926 until his death.

It seems incredible that numbers of these children, the majority of whom are born and bred in Gloucester, were hitherto unconscious of the existence of a cathedral in the heart of their city, and a still greater number, although acquainted with its existence, had never been inside it. When asked where the Cathedral was, one promising youth said he thought it was "at the back of the Palladium," which is significant, the Palladium being a cinema.[6] Another small child exclaimed to its teacher as they entered the precincts, "Why, teacher, it looks like a church!"

The following is the programme with notes which was performed at the series of recitals in 1924:

1. *Romanza* (from the Symphony
   'La Reine de France')[7]   ...   .   Haydn

Franz Joseph Haydn was born in 1732. It is said that he practised 16 hours a day. At the early age of six he was sent away to school, and he sadly missed his mother's care. Writing of his school-days he says: "I could not help perceiving, much to my distress, that I was gradually getting very dirty. I was not always able to avoid spots of dirt on my clothes, of which I was dreadfully ashamed – in fact I was a regular little urchin." He was a great friend of Mozart. His best-known work is *The Creation*, which was produced in 1798, and was first performed at a Gloucester Festival in 1802. He died in 1809, the year Mendelssohn was born.

2. Fugue in D minor[8]   ...   .   Bach

This fugue is known as 'The Giant', and probably called so because of the stately figure which appears only in the bass (the pedal part), and it is easily recognized by its strength and massiveness. Try and note the number of times the 'Giant' enters. Bach was one of the greatest composers that ever lived. He was born in 1685 and died in 1750. His family was a large one; he had no less than 20 children.

---

6   The Palladium, an early silent cinema, was converted from a shop in Westgate Street in 1913.
7   Symphony No.85 in B flat (second movement).
8   This is the prelude on the chorale *Wir glauben all' an einen Gott* (BWV 680).

3. Solo *Holy, Holy*[9] ... ... Handel

George Frederick Handel was born in 1685 and died in 1759. His best-known work is *The Messiah*, which he composed in 24 days. It has always been included in the programme of the Gloucester Festivals.[10]

4. One of the Gloucester Cathedral Chimes ... John Stephens

The four tunes played on the bells should be quite familiar to all Gloucester children, but it is feared they are not so well known as they ought to be. The one included in the programme is by an old Cathedral Chorister – Dr John Stephens. He was born in Gloucester in 1720. In 1746 he became Organist of Salisbury Cathedral, and held that post till his death in 1780. He conducted the Gloucester Festival in 1766. The chime has been arranged for the piano by Mr Lee Williams (Organist of the Cathedral, 1882–97), and transcribed for the organ by Dr Brewer. The final movement is a fugue. Note the number of entries of the chime as in the 'Giant' fugue by Bach.

5. Hymn – *When I survey the wondrous cross.*

The tune 'Rockingham' was written by Edward Miller. Born 1735, died 1807.

6. Choral Prelude on 'Rockingham' ... ... C. H. H. Parry

This Prelude is written on the above hymn tune 'Rockingham'. Try and follow the tune throughout the Prelude. Sir Hubert Parry lived at Highnam, a village just outside Gloucester. He wrote many beautiful works for the Gloucester Festivals. He was born in 1848 and died in 1918.

7. Minuet from the Symphony in E flat[11] ... ... Mozart

Mozart was born in 1756. He showed his love for music in such a remarkable manner when he was only three, that his father taught

---

9   The aria 'Ombra mai fu', from Handel's opera *Serse*, popularly known then as Handel's 'Largo'.
10 With the exception of 1955 the tradition of including *Messiah* at Three Choirs Festivals was maintained until the 1963 Worcester Festival. It was not heard again until the 250th Festival at Gloucester in 1977.
11 Symphony No.39 (K.543).

him to play at that early age. He was composing his beautiful *Requiem* when he died in 1791, and he never actually completed it. He told his wife that he was writing it for himself.

8. Pomp and Circumstance (March)[12]...   ...   .   Elgar

Sir Edward Elgar is the greatest living composer, and was born at Worcester 1857. His greatest choral work is *The Dream of Gerontius*, which has been sung in Gloucester on many occasions. The middle section of the March is well known to everybody as the tune of 'Land of Hope and Glory'. It is taken from his Coronation Ode, which he wrote for the Coronation of King Edward VII.

One Verse of the National Anthem.

The composer of this tune is said to be Dr John Bull,[13] born in 1562 and died in 1628, but nothing seems to have been heard of the tune until it was sung at a dinner in 1740 to celebrate the taking of Portobello by Admiral Vernon.

During the singing of the hymn I conduct and my assistant plays.

---

12   No.1.
13   The theory that Bull (1562–1628) composed the music of the National Anthem has
     long been discredited.

– 18 –

More reminiscences

I suppose there is no subject about which people in general know so little and yet affect to know so much, as music. If the many 'howlers' made in connection with it were not so humorous they would be indeed pitiable. At the moment I am thinking of a lady at the Hereford Festival in 1921, who conscientiously followed through the score of Rossini's *Stabat Mater* when Dvořák's setting was being performed, and afterwards was heard to say that it was one of the chief pleasures of the Festival. On another occasion I sat next to an elderly lady, who, during the singing of the *Hallelujah* chorus, followed first of all the soprano line with her finger, then the alto line and then the tenor and bass, and by the time she had reached the bottom of the first page the chorus had finished. She then turned to her companion, and in an audible whisper said, "Why don't they do it all?"

Another peculiarity about music, or rather the musical profession, is that so many people seem unable to grasp the fact that it is a profession, and expect musicians to be willing, one might almost say eager, to entertain their friends. Some years ago I came into possession of a letter written by Sims Reeves,[1] who evidently resented this attitude of the public mind towards music, and which, I feel, is worth reproducing.

> 99 Inverness Terrace
> Kensington Gardens
> July 7, 1859

> Dear Sir
> I am entirely at a loss to understand your letter. I do not sing at Dinners except on extraordinary occasions, and then my terms are fifty guineas.

---

1 (John) Sims Reeves (1818–1900), the opera and music hall singer, was the dedicatee of Sullivan's song 'Sigh no more, ladies'. It was said that "It is probable that Sims Reeves lost more money through unfulfilled engagements than any other singer that ever lived."

Having purchased a ticket it was my intention to do myself the pleasure of dining with my friend Charles Kean[2] on the occasion mentioned.

Should I however be called upon to sing I beg most distinctly to decline and to beg that my guinea be returned when the ticket will be delivered up.

I am, Sir,
Your obedient servant
J. Sims Reeves

There is no beating about the bush here, and musicians will approve the sentiment so forcibly conveyed in this letter. An unpleasant truth that has to be faced sometimes by musicians is the fact that 'music soothes the savage breast',[3] or to put it more correctly the 'crazed' breast, for musical services appear to have a special attraction for poor demented souls who show an inclination to attach themselves particularly to cathedrals. My own experience in this connection was with a member of my Coventry choir, who, after a lengthy period of absence from the church, called on me one day to explain his non-attendance. He told me that he had been ill with influenza, and had lost his voice and could not speak. He went on to say that he had prayed earnestly for his voice to be restored. "But," said he, "my prayer was misunderstood. I prayed for my speaking voice, but I have been given a most beautiful singing voice and I want you to test it now." I saw at once that the poor fellow had lost his mental balance. I humoured him, and after hearing him attempt to sing a few notes I advised him to take the greatest possible care of his voice, and not to use it except on extraordinary occasions. In this way I got him without difficulty out of the house. This was the last time I saw him, for he died soon after in a lunatic asylum.

There is also the person who raves about some particular performer or composer, the sort of fanatic Dr Davan Wetton[4]

---

2   Charles Kean (1811–68), actor and theatrical impresario.
3   This is a common misquotation from the opening line of William Congreve's play *The Mourning Bride* (1697). Congreve actually wrote "Musick has Charms to sooth a savage Breast".
4   Brewer incorrectly refers to Dr Henry Davan Wetton as 'Dr *Davon* Wetton'. Rosalie Davan Wetton – Dr Davan Wetton's daughter – was sometime organist of Girton College, Cambridge, and, like Brewer, was a former pupil of Sir Walter Parratt.

encountered at the Foundling Hospital. His account of that experience is well worth repeating. Whilst playing there one day he heard the rustle of skirts behind him. He stopped and looked round to see who the intruder might be. It was a lady who had found her way into the organ-loft and was gazing at the keys. "Excuse me," she said, and her accent betrayed her American origin, "is this the organ George Frederick Handel played on?" "Yes," said Dr Wetton. "I couldn't go back to America without coming to see the organ George Frederick Handel played on. Will you kindly allow me to kiss the keys?" Her request was readily granted. "But," Dr Wetton said to me, "I didn't tell her that they were new keys put in a few years ago." Not seemingly in a hurry to leave, the lady from across the Atlantic informed my friend that she was a great admirer of all George Frederick Handel's works, and asked if she might beg one more favour. She would so like, when she went back to America, to be able to tell her friends that she had sung one of George Frederick Handel's solos, and had accompanied herself on the same instrument he played on. Permission was given, and she thereupon sat at the keyboard and sang 'O rest in the Lord'![5]

---

5   From Mendelssohn's *Elijah*!

– 19 –

The post-war revival (1920–22)

A ll who were associated with the Three Choirs Festivals were most anxious for their revival as soon as possible after the long lapse during the war. Gloucester had held the last in 1913. There was such keenness amongst the choral members that each of the three cities wanted to lead off in 1920, but as it was Worcester's turn, and the year in which the Worcester Festival would have been held had there been no war, it naturally fell to its lot to revive them. There were certain officials connected with Worcester who were very nervous about carrying on the Festival on the same lines as before. Their idea was to limit it to one-half the time, and also reduce the expenses by one-half, but wiser counsels prevailed and the Three Choirs 'carried on' as if there had been no break. It took very little time to set the machinery in motion, the organization of these ancient meetings being so well established that they work almost automatically.

The gap in the conductorship at Hereford caused by Dr Sinclair's death was filled by the appointment of his assistant Dr Percy Hull, who had spent the whole of his musical life either as a chorister or assistant in Hereford Cathedral, and so had imbibed the traditions of the festivals. This was indeed fortunate not only for Hereford but also for Gloucester and Worcester.[1]

At this Worcester Festival in 1920 Beethoven's *Three Equali* for four trombones was included in the programme and played in memory of Parry, Lloyd and Sinclair, all of whom had died since the last Festival in 1913. This I conducted in the Lady Chapel, as Sir Ivor Atkins could not leave the conductor's post in the nave. It was at this Festival that Gervase Elwes sang for the last time. As I wished him and Lady Winifride good-bye at the close of the Festival he told me

---

1   Hull (1878–1968) was knighted in 1947 for services to music, especially for his work in reviving the Three Choirs Festival after the Second World War.

that it was his intention to retire from the profession on his return from his approaching tour in America. "And I am going with him to take care of him," added Lady Winifride as we separated. Little did we realize what an ill-fated trip it was to prove.[2]

A wish was expressed by the citizens of Worcester that their poorer brethren should have an opportunity of hearing the festival choir after the performance of the *Messiah*. The chorus readily fell in with this suggestion, and the *Hallelujah* chorus and *Worthy is the Lamb* were sung outside the cathedral on the spot now occupied by the war memorial. It should be put on record, too, that when the brass players of the London Symphony Orchestra heard of the proposal they most generously came forward and gave their services. This spontaneous gift on the part of the executants of the Festival was greatly appreciated by a vast concourse of people assembled in and outside the cathedral precincts, and by none more so than the many ragged little urchins who came under my notice. Who can tell what far-reaching effect it will have on those young minds?

There was little new music produced at the Hereford Festival in 1921, the only novelties in the cathedral being *Heaven's Gate* by Walford Davies and *The Paling of the Stars* by B. J. Dale,[3] and at the first secular concert W. H. Reed's *Lincoln Imp*, that exceedingly clever work which has found its way into many festival schemes since its production,[4] and my Pastorals for tenor solo and orchestra, *Jillian of Berry*. I was fortunate again on this occasion in having that great artist John Coates to introduce them. Another feature at this Festival was the inclusion of a Wesley anthem at each of the Three Choirs Services at Evensong.

It may not be generally understood that the Festivals, although styled 'Three Choirs', are not governed by a committee drawn from the three cities, but each city organizes its own Festival, bears the

---

2   Gervase Elwes (1866–1921) died from injuries sustained in a railway accident at Back Bay railway station, Boston, while travelling to an engagement at Harvard University. The Memorial Fund established in his name became the Musicians Benevolent Fund in 1930. Elgar, who regarded Elwes as the outstanding interpreter of the role of Gerontius, was deeply affected by Elwes's death, and agreed to become the first President of the Memorial Fund.
3   Benjamin James Dale (1885–1943) was Warden of the Royal Academy of Music.
4   It was repeated at the 1922 (Gloucester) and 1930 (Hereford) festivals.

financial responsibility of it, and arranges the programme. The conditions of stewardship vary. The preparation of the chorus, however, is different, each organist being responsible for the selection and training of his own contingent for every Festival. The profits and collections are also divided equally amongst the three dioceses. The organist of the cathedral at which the Festival is held conducts, the other organists playing the organ at the morning and evening performances respectively.

The outside world probably does not realize the enormous amount of enthusiasm required from both singers and conductors. Not only has the *yearly* Festival to be prepared for, but during the winter season, in Gloucester alone, a town of some 60,000 inhabitants, no less than seven musical societies are holding their weekly rehearsals. This means that chorus singers in each place have a minimum amount of rest from singing – a few weeks only throughout the year. Too much praise, therefore, cannot be given them – the hardest workers of the Festivals – for the ungrudging way they give up the delightful summer evenings to prepare for these Festivals. It proves their loyalty to their conductor and their enthusiasm for their work.

In the midst of the heavy work entailed in the preparation for the 1922 Festival I thought it would be good for all concerned to have a day off, and so I invited the members of my own contingent, some two hundred strong, to a picnic. The Dean and some of the Canons accompanied us. What changes have taken place since the days when a Canon's wife was heard to say she often saw Mr — (one of the Minor Canons) going to his work, but she didn't know him! The spirit of democracy since those days has fortunately crept even into the precincts of cathedral cities, and those whose duties are in such places are all the happier for it. I have worked in the past with members of a capitular body who did not even know the names of the lay-clerks, although some had been singing in the choir for nearly twenty years. It is inconceivable, but nevertheless true. But I am digressing.

Unfortunately the day chosen for the picnic was not as fine as we could have wished, but even the dampness of the day did not damp the ardour of those who journeyed by motor over the Cotswold Hills. Halts were made at various interesting spots, at Seven Springs, the source of the Thames; at Birdlip, the highest point of the Cotswolds, where we had tea at the Royal George Hotel; and Painswick. It was at Painswick, it will be remembered, that I had in my youth the experience of the pea-shooting boys.[5] In the churchyard are a number of very fine yew trees. Report says that there are ninety-nine, and that in spite of repeated efforts the hundredth will never grow. I had made arrangements to show the chorus this old-world village and church. When we arrived I found the church full of people, and fearing that I had happened upon an unexpected service I tiptoed out of the building, so as not to disturb the congregation. On making inquiries I was told, "Dr Brewer is going to bring his festival chorus to sing in the church!"

Naturally this information came as a great surprise, as I had not divulged my plans, but as the inhabitants of the village had turned out in such numbers I thought it would be a great disappointment to them if they did not hear some singing, so I ventured to suggest that if they came out of the church and let us go in (the chorus filled it easily) we would sing for their benefit. This they did, and the chorus sang Bach's sublime motet *Now shall the grace*[6] in a way which must have been a revelation to these country folk, some of whom, possibly, had never heard the name of Bach. After the singing I was asked to play some Bach on the organ, but I doubt whether this request would have been made had the vicar known how I should condemn the instrument after playing on it!

It is lamentable to think how much money collected by strenuous efforts, mainly in small sums, is thrown away on inferior organs, and how sensitive nerves are tortured and services marred by the same. The spending of the money is usually in the hands of well-meaning but inexperienced and unpractical enthusiasts, who are attracted by quantity rather than quality, and fail to realize the necessity for obtaining expert advice.

Since our last Festival in 1913 many of the prominent Stewards and officials had died, including the Chairman of the Executive Committee. Since his retirement in 1896 my friend and predecessor, Lee Williams, had consistently done everything in his power to

5   See p.8 above.
6   This is not one of Bach's six *bona fide* motets (BWV 225–30), but Cantata No.50 (*Nun ist das heil*), comprising a single movement for double chorus (8vv.) and instruments.

further the cause of music, and especially in connection with the Three Choirs. For some years he had taken up his abode on the outskirts of Gloucester, and when the chairmanship became vacant he was invited to accept the position, and it gave immense satisfaction to all concerned when he willingly complied. This closer relationship between us cemented more than ever the great friendship which had existed for the long period of fifty years, from the time when as a boy I sang under his conductorship at Llandaff in the Madrigal Society.[7] He gave me the most loyal support, and I am greatly indebted to him not only for his valuable help as Chairman, but for the support he has extended to me throughout my occupation of the organistship of the Cathedral.

It was my desire to make the 1922 Festival essentially British, and in the programme appeared no less than twenty-seven works by British composers. The complete programme was as follows:

Sunday Afternoon

Elegiac Variations on an original theme	T. F. Dunhill
(Dedicated to the Memory of Sir Hubert Parry)	
Magnificat and Nunc Dimittis in C	A. Herbert Brewer
In te Domine speravi (Prelude)[8]	J. W. G. Hathaway
Anthem 'How Lovely'	Brahms
Anthem *Thou wilt keep him*	C. Lee Williams
Symphony in C minor (Last movement)	Brahms

Tuesday Morning

New Work – *Sine Nomine*	Herbert Howells
(Phantasy for Orchestra with Organ)	
The Lord's Prayer (Unaccompanied Motet)	C. Lee Williams
Elijah	Mendelssohn

Tuesday Evening

The Apostles	Edward Elgar

---

7   Lee Williams had been organist of Llandaff Cathedral from 1876 to 1882.
8   This Prelude (for strings, brass, organ and drums) had been composed for the 1907 Gloucester festival. In the same year an organ arrangement by Brewer was published by Novello & Co. Ltd.

Wednesday Morning

The Kingdom	Edward Elgar
Symphony in D	Brahms
Motet – 'Now shall the grace'	Bach
New Work: Prelude and First Part	Bantock
(From *The Song of Songs*)	

*Unveiling of the Tablet to the Memory of
Charles Hubert Hastings Parry
by
The Right Hon. Viscount Gladstone*

Ode, *Blest Pair of Sirens*	C. H. H. Parry

Wednesday Evening

Symphonic Variations	C. H. H. Parry
'Vorspiel' and 'Liebestod' (*Tristan und Isolde*)	Wagner
Two Orchestral Pieces:	Edward German
(a) *The Willow Song* (Othello)	
(b) *Harvest Dance* (from *The Seasons*)	
Songs:	I. A. Atkins
(a) *The Shepherdess*	
(b) *Thou art come*	
A Whimsical Phantasy for Orchestra,	W. H. Reed
The Lincoln Imp	
Songs:	Granville Bantock
(a) *The March*	
(b) *The Emperor*	
(a) *Danse Sacrée*	Debussy
(b) *Danse Profane*	
Song – 'Ave Maria'	Max Bruch
Capriccio Espagnol	Rimsky-Korsakov

Thursday Morning

Le Poème de L'Extase	Scriabin
Ode to Music	C. H. H. Parry
Motet – *There is an old belief*	C. H. H. Parry
New Work – *Colour Symphony*	A. Bliss

New Work – *Silence*[9]   Eugene Goossens[10]
Two Psalms[11]   G. Holst
Requiem   Verdi

Thursday Evening

Fantasia and Fugue in C minor[12]   Bach
     (Transcribed by Edward Elgar. First performance of the Fantasia)[13]
The Holy Innocents   A. Herbert Brewer
     (Revised for this Festival)
Symphony No.3 in E flat ('Eroica')   Beethoven
Selections from *Judas Maccabæus*   Handel
For the Fallen[14]   Edward Elgar
Last Post (Choral Song)   C. V. Stanford

Friday

The Messiah   Handel

This was the first Gloucester Festival since Hubert Parry's death, and it was felt that there should be some marked recognition of the man and his art. The Dean and Chapter had already sanctioned the erection of a tablet in the Cathedral to his memory, and it was therefore decided that the opportunity should be taken of unveiling the tablet during the week, and the event proved to be one of the most impressive features of the Festival. The ceremony was simple and appropriate. A procession was formed of musicians in their doctors' robes, who, with the Bishop and Dean, proceeded to where the tablet is placed on the west wall of the south aisle. Lord

---

9   A 'choral fragment' for choir and orchestra.
10 Sir (Aynsley) Eugene Goossens (1893–1962), son of the violinist and conductor Eugène Goossens (1867–1958).
11 Psalms 86 and 148, although Holst's setting of 'Psalm 148' appears not to draw on the text of the Psalm itself.
12 BWV 537.
13 Under an arrangement agreed between Elgar and Richard Strauss in 1920, the latter was to have orchestrated the Fantasia, though he never fulfilled the deed. Elgar's orchestration of the Fugue had been given its first performance at the Queen's Hall, London, under Eugène Goossens in October 1921. The Gloucester premiere of the complete work was conducted by Elgar.
14 From *The Spirit of England*, Op.80.

Gladstone, Sir Edward Elgar, Sir Charles Stanford, Sir Hugh Allen,[15] Sir Henry Hadow, Professor Granville Bantock, and Dr Brewer took part in this procession. The tablet was formally presented to the Cathedral and unveiled. The Bishop[16] read a couple of prayers, and then Lord Gladstone, returning to the conductor's desk, spoke to the congregation of what Parry had been in the musical life of his time, and of his character as a man. Lord Gladstone was at Eton with Parry as a boy, and perhaps the most remarkable passage in his speech was one in which he told how the "freshness, vigour, sincerity, fervour, idealism" of Parry's personality swept the Eton boys from prejudice and disregard of the arts into a loving admiration. The qualities of the boy, he said, remained those of the man through life, as the inscription of the Poet Laureate records on the tablet placed in the Cathedral.[17]

The proceedings concluded with an inspiring performance of *Blest Pair of Sirens* under the direction of Sir Hugh Allen, Parry's successor at the Royal College of Music. Two letters of interest in connection with the unveiling of the memorial reached me in reply to invitations to the Poet Laureate and Sir Walter Parratt to be present. Dr Robert Bridges[18] writes:

Chilswell
Oxford
August 25, 1922

Dear Dr Brewer

Personally I very much regret that I cannot accept your most kind and attractive invitation – and I wish I could come to Gloucester and renew my old memories of the Cathedral and once again drink in the music of your

---

15 Sir Hugh Allen (1869–1946) was concurrently Professor of Music at Oxford and Director of the Royal College of Music (both 1918–46).

16 The Rt Rev'd Edgar Gibson (1848–1924).

17 The original edition of *Memories of Choirs and Cloisters* includes a group photograph taken on the occasion for *The Times*, showing Stanford and Elgar seated at opposite ends of the front row. Stanford had entertained a long-standing animosity towards Elgar, and the two were barely on speaking terms. At the unveiling of the Parry Memorial Tablet Brewer persuaded the two to shake hands. An account of the quarrel is given in Jeremy Dibble, *C. Hubert H. Parry: His Life and Music* (Oxford, 1992), pp.401–2.

18 Robert Bridges (1844–1930) was Poet Laureate from 1913 until his death.

delicate fingering – and besides, I should wish to take my part in honouring my old friend Parry: but I have more work on hand than I can get through, and cannot spare the days from it. And after all I am better away, because the tablet in the Cathedral is not what I wished it to be, and my disappointment and dissatisfaction, which I should not well disguise, would be out of place.

Yours truly
Robert Bridges

Sir Walter Parratt replied:

Worthing
August 22, 1922

My dear Brewer

I am here with my wife and three daughters, and I should find it very awkward to get away. My Spirit will be with you. Festival fever does not suit me.

The little birds which do not sing in scales delight my ears. The airs on these downs are the best music.

How we miss Lloyd!

Yours ever
Walter Parratt

In addition to the performance of Parry's works mentioned in the programme, the *Elegiac Variations*, specially written as a memorial to him by Dunhill, were played at the opening service; and a *Fantasie* for the organ on Parry's hymn tune *Intercessor*, also written in memory of him by Stanford, was performed at the close of one of the evening services. This organ solo, with others specially written by W. H. Reed and Basil Harwood, formed a feature at the daily services of the three cathedral choirs.

The performance of *The Kingdom* might almost be described as a revival of that work, for it had not been given by the Three Choirs since the Worcester Festival in 1908. In speaking of the choir's singing in *The Kingdom* Mr Colles[19] in *The Times* said:

---

19 H. C. Colles (1879–1943), a pupil of Parry, succeeded J. A. Fuller-Maitland (1856–1936) as chief music critic of *The Times* in 1911, and held the post until his death.

It is generally agreed that the Three Choirs Festival
has a choir this year second to none in its history, and,
listening from a seat at the west end of the Cathedral, it
was certainly the choral tone which made every climax
the thrilling event that it was. But it is not only weight
of tone, but precision, neatness of attack and rhythmic
resilience, in which this choir excels. Elgar has set them
many awkward passages to sing. There are places where
the ensemble seems unnecessarily intricate as a means of
expression, but the singers were scarcely ever at fault. A
momentary loss of pitch by the men's voices in the chorus
"When the great Lord" was practically the only technical
lapse, and it was a small one. The clearness of the several
parts in the cry of the multitude, "What meaneth this,"
was a triumph of good training and intelligent singing.

Certainly no conductor could have wished for a more loyal and
enthusiastic chorus. It was not until a fortnight before the Festival
that the copies of Goossens' work, *Silence*, were placed in their
hands, but so anxious were they to give of their best that the
Gloucester contingent consented to a daily rehearsal in order to
become acquainted with it.

The Stewards had invited me to compose something new, but
owing to the enormous amount of work in connection with the
revival of the Festival I could not find the time, and decided to revise
The Holy Innocents, which was written for the Festival of 1904.
This was included in the Thursday evening programme, which, in a
sense, might be described as a war memorial performance, including
as it did amongst other works Elgar's *For the Fallen* and Stanford's
Last Post. The production of Elgar's transcription of Bach's Fantasia
in C minor, played in conjunction with his brilliant arrangement of
the Fugue, was a memorable item in this programme, which proved
to be the most attractive in point of numbers of the week, no less
than 3,619 seats having been booked, thus constituting a record for
the Three Choirs. In fact the whole Festival surpassed any other in
the annals of the Three Choirs. The enormous sum of £2,100 was
available for the Charity, and the attendances outdistanced all others. It is interesting to compare the figures of the three consecutive
Festivals since their revival after the war:

Worcester, 1920	Hereford, 1921	Gloucester, 1922
10,521	9,588	17,357

Even the weather achieved a record. Although fine weather during the Festivals has been a tradition, that particular summer was so wet that it was nothing short of a miracle to have seven successive fine days. Rain fell within a few miles of Gloucester, but not a drop fell in the city. A provincial paper, in speaking of the Festival, says:[20] "The Gloucester Festival happily finds Dr Brewer where he was in 191. [*sic*]" I might have exclaimed as did Mark Twain, when he received a telegram asking if the report that he was dead was true, "Grossly exaggerated!"

---

20 This observation, taken 'From a Midland journal', is quoted by Herbert Thompson at the conclusion of his extended review of the 1922 Gloucester festival, in Herbert Thompson, 'The Gloucester Musical Festival', *Musical Times*, 63 (1922), pp.705–9, at p.708. Thompson wryly comments: "Happily, indeed; but then Cathedral organists are notoriously a long-lived race."!

1922: City High Sheriff and politics

S oon after the Festival of 1922 a deputation waited on me on behalf of the members of the City Council, with a request that I would accept the office of City High Sheriff. As this was the unanimous wish of Conservative, Liberal and Labour parties alike, I consented. It was, as far as I know, the first time that an active cathedral organist had been offered the post, though when invested with the robe and chain of office at the council meeting I could not refrain from reminding the City Aldermen and Councillors that, although Gloucester led the way in many things, this was not the first time the art of music had been recognized by a Mayor and Corporation; they would all remember how the Pied Piper of Hamelin had been called in to rid that city of rats; and even in regard to rats Gloucester was somewhat akin to that city in that during the recent Festival, for the first time within living memory, rats had appeared in the cathedral. Fortunately the ladies of the chorus were unaware of the fact. They made their temporary home immediately underneath the singers on the orchestra, no doubt attracted there by the music, and not by the organ "bellace" as on that far-off occasion in 1667.[1]

Happily the duties during my year of office did not entail the awful necessity of witnessing the execution of the extreme penalty of the law; in fact so free was the city from crime during that period that I was placed in the unique position of having to present to the Judge of Assize on two consecutive occasions a pair of white gloves as a symbol of the purity and freedom of the city from crime. On the second occasion my Under Sheriff forgot to bring the gloves to the Assize Court, although great care had been taken to obtain the right size. The result was that after congratulating the city on having no cases for trial and asking his lordship's acceptance of a pair of white gloves, no gloves were forthcoming for me to present – a situation

---

1   See above, p.11. At the 1962 Gloucester Three Choirs Festival the present editor occupied seats with a clear view under the chorus staging. Rats were very much in evidence then too.

which caused much amusement to his lordship and to the Court, and much discomfort to myself. However, his lordship good-humouredly said he hoped to receive them on a future occasion, and the omission was rectified during the luncheon interval.

The office of City High Sheriff is of very ancient origin and dates back to 1483, and I believe I am right in saying that only in three other cities in England does the office of City High Sheriff exist – London, Winchester and Exeter. The position of Master of the Choristers is also an office of long standing, and came into existence in 1544. When receiving the congratulations of the choristers on my new appointment I explained to them the duties of High Sheriff and, in concluding my remarks, asked the smallest boy in the choir what would happen to them if they sang badly on the following Sunday, when the High Sheriff would accompany the Judge to the cathedral and conduct the anthem. Trembling in his shoes the small boy gasped out, "Please, sir, you'll hang us!"

One of my first duties during my year of office was to declare the poll to some thousands of people after the election in 1923. I elected to perform this duty on a megaphone, but, judging from the cat calls and general pandemonium which ensued, my performance did not give general satisfaction. Only on one other occasion was I associated with political activities. It was during the war, in the spring of 1916. Lord Quenington,[2] who was member for the Tewkesbury Division of Gloucestershire, lost his life in Egypt when the Gloucestershire Yeomanry suffered so heavily, and his death necessitated an election for that Division. At that time the 'wait and see' policy of the Government was causing an immense amount of dissatisfaction throughout the country, and it was felt that business men were needed in Parliament to carry the war to a successful issue. Mr William Boosey was the first on the scene, and he came forward as an independent candidate promising, if elected, to resign at the end of the war that the seat might then be contested by the older political parties. Calling on me when he came to Gloucester he propounded his views, and expressed the hope that I would propose him. Little did I realize how the fat would be in the fire when I consented. His address was sent out, and he began working

---

2   Michael Hugh Hicks-Beach (1877–1916).

energetically before the older parties decided on their course of action. Eventually the choice of the Conservatives fell on Lord Quenington's uncle, Mr W. F. Hicks-Beach,[3] brother to the late Earl St Aldwyn.[4] The Liberals did not bring forward a candidate. My friends on all sides were shocked at my supporting Mr Boosey in opposition to one who was so beloved throughout the county, and with whom I was also on very friendly terms, and for mixing myself up with politics at all.

The London Press had much to say about this by-election. The *Daily Mail* mentioned that "Mr. Boosey had the strong support of Dr. Brewer who carried great weight in the county." On the other hand the *Daily News* contemptuously remarked:

> The poverty of Mr Boosey's candidature, from the local point of view, was apparent by his lack of influential support at the nominations – Dr Brewer, the cathedral organist, being his only notable capture. Mr Boosey's friendship with distinguished musicians is a very pleasant thing personally, but why on earth it should be brought to bear on the question of bringing the country victoriously through the biggest war in history only those who are determined to worry the Government simply because it is the Government can say.

When the election fever was at its height the late Bishop Mitchinson,[5] Master of Pembroke College, Oxford, and Canon of Gloucester Cathedral, wrote me the following letter:

Pembroke College
Oxford
May 12, 1916

Dear Dr Brewer
    I rejoiced greatly to see that you had had the patriotic pluck to propose Boosey. Till Asquith,[6] who is an

---

3   William Frederick Hicks-Beach (1841–1923).
4   Michael Edward Hicks-Beach (1837–1916), created Earl St Aldwyn in 1915.
5   Bishop John Mitchinson (1833–1918).
6   Herbert Henry Asquith (1852–1928) served as Liberal Prime Minister from 1908 to 1916.

incorrigible political intriguer, is driven from power, I am hopeless as to the outcome of the war.

No acknowledgment is desired by your friend now of 17 years,

J. Mitchinson

Mr Hicks-Beach was supported by both Conservatives and Liberals, and so won the seat by some 1,500 votes.[7]

Parry, who was a staunch Liberal, delighted in repeating a story of an old coachman at Highnam who used to drive the family about in a waggonette. On the occasion in question the waggonette was occupied by Lady Maud[8] and a friend. The coachman could not help overhearing the conversation of the two ladies sitting behind him. Both were keen politicians, and discussed politics throughout the drive. When they had returned to Highnam Court and were dismounting from the waggonette the coachman, who was an ardent Tory, turned to them and said, "I've 'eard what you two ladies 'ave been talkin' about, but thank God you aint got any votes." I wonder what the old coachman – if he is still alive – thinks of the women's vote now!

---

7   Hicks-Beach defeated Boosey by 7,127 to 5,689.
8   Lady Parry, the composer's wife.

– 21 –

1923–5

The year 1923 being the tercentenary of Byrd and Weelkes special attention was drawn to these composers at the Worcester Festival by the inclusion of motets and string music by them in the Wednesday programme. For the first time at Worcester, and following the example of Hereford, an extra concert was given in the College Hall[1] on the Friday night in which a small number of the London Symphony Orchestra took part.

During the year 1924 the world of music suffered the loss of three very distinguished musicians – Stanford, Parratt and Frederick Bridge, and it was in memory of them that the *Three Equali* by Beethoven were played at the opening of the Hereford Festival. Again on this occasion it was my privilege to conduct those fine artists, the trombonists of the London Symphony Orchestra, but this time they were placed under the orchestra, and the effect was hardly as satisfactory as when played in the distant Lady Chapel at Worcester.

There was little novelty heard on this occasion, only three short works appearing in the programme – *The Tower* by Edgar Bainton, performed in the cathedral, and two at the first secular concert – *Æsop's Fables* by W. H. Reed and a miniature suite for voice and orchestra, *Miller's Green*, which I had been asked to write.[2]

In the course of the preparations for the 1925 Festival at Gloucester I revived the question of the entertainment tax,[3] but I did not get much sympathy or support from many members of the Executive Committee, their argument being that both Worcester and Hereford had tried to get exemption and had failed in their endeavours. The tax was regarded as an iniquitous one, especially as the entire profits

---

1 The monastic refectory, now leased to the King's School.
2 Millers Green is that part of the Cathedral precincts where the Organist's house is situated. Brewer's punctuation has been retained here. See p.15, fn.21.
3 An entertainment tax was introduced as part of the Finance (New Duties) Act and Finance Act of 1916. The rates were reduced in 1920 after strong protests, but the tax was not abolished until 1960.

of these music meetings were handed to the Charity. I was told that it would mean waste of time and money to go to London to make the attempt, but I still pressed the matter. Finally a small committee was appointed to interview the government officials, consisting of the Member for Gloucester, Colonel Horlick;[4] the Treasurer of the Diocesan Board, Major Birchall;[5] the Secretary, Mr Alan Jones, and myself. Our efforts were not in vain; I was able to satisfy the officials on all the points required, chiefly as regards the permanency of these ancient Festivals; we gained our object, and were granted exemption from the tax, thus achieving a saving of nearly £1,000 on our previous Festival in 1922.

Invitations to write new works had been accepted by Sibelius, Gustav Holst,[6] Charles Wood,[7] J. B. McEwen,[8] Walford Davies,[9] Basil Harwood,[10] Herbert Howells[11] and others, including myself. In all there were no less than ten new works, an advance in novelties over any other Festival. It was also essentially an English programme, for there were thirty-four different British composers represented in the scheme. The enormous attendances proved that the Committee were justified in their policy as regards novelties as well as the programme generally. The *Messiah* drew the largest number: the tickets sold were 3,410. The total attendances for the week amounted to 19,973, which was a record for the Three Choirs Festivals. This figure did not include those who were present at the Sunday opening service, when the congregation must have numbered between four and five thousand, or at the daily services. The collections totalled £826, and a sum of no less than £3,700 was available for the Charity, £1,600 more than the previous record at these Festivals, which was at Gloucester in 1922.

Apart from the achievement of such records there were other features which helped to make this Festival historical. The

---

4 Lieutenant-Colonel Sir James Nockells Horlick (1886–1972), 4th Baronet, who was MP for Gloucester from 1923 to 1929.
5 Major – later 'Sir' – John D. Birchall (1875–1941), a Major in the Royal Gloucestershire Hussars, served as MP for Leeds North East from 1918 to 1940.
6 *The Evening Watch*, for tenor and contralto soloists and unaccompanied choir.
7 The anthem *Glory and Honour and Laud*.
8 *Prelude for Orchestra*.
9 *Men and Angels*, for chorus and orchestra.
10 *Love Incarnate*, for chorus and orchestra.
11 *Paradise Rondel*, for orchestra.

appearance of Dame Ethel Smyth as a composer and conductor in the Cathedral and Shire Hall. For the Cathedral two numbers from her *Mass in D* had been chosen,[12] and the overture, *The Wreckers*, for the Shire Hall. It was not the first time that a woman composer had appeared at a Three Choirs Festival; as has already been mentioned, Miss Ellicott figured in at least two Festival programmes at Gloucester,[13] but this was the first occasion on which a woman composer had been heard or seen as a conductor in a cathedral.

Unfortunately Sibelius was unable to finish his promised Symphony[14] or to visit Gloucester, so the Brahms Variations on the chorale *St Antoni* was substituted.[15] When it was first announced that Sibelius had consented to write a work for Gloucester and that he would visit England purposely to conduct it, a scribe from a well-known provincial paper called on me to ask if I would give him the address of the 'lady' who was writing the new Symphony as he wished to ask her for her photograph to publish in his paper, and he added, "Of course Sibelius is this lady's *nom de plume*?"![16]

This being the tercentenary of Orlando Gibbons a motet by him was included in all the programmes except one, when time would not permit of its inclusion.[17] His name figured so prominently that attention was naturally drawn to him, which led to an amusing episode in the form of letters addressed to Orlando Gibbons care of me, with a request that they should be forwarded! They were from various agencies wanting to do business with him! Other features which should be mentioned were the broadcasting of the two secular concerts,[18] and the unveiling by Sir Hugh Allen of a tablet in the Shire Hall recording Parry's generous gift of the gallery, which

---

12   The *Kyrie* and *Gloria*.
13   See above, p.63, fn.2.
14   This was presumably the elusive Symphony No.8, which was completed in 1929. It was apparently destroyed by the composer in 1945, without having ever been performed.
15   Sibelius's symphonic poem *Finlandia* (Op.26) was performed also.
16   The confusion was presumably prompted by the composer's forename 'Jean'.
17   The works described by Brewer as 'motets' are, of course, English anthems, viz. *O clap your hands*, *God is gone up* (the second part of *O clap your hands*) and *Hosanna to the Son of David*.
18   The broadcasts came about through the influence of Brewer's elder son Charles, who was a member of the BBC production staff at the time. His autobiography *The Spice of Variety* was published in 1948.

has already been referred to in connection with the 1910 Festival. Sir Hugh, after the unveiling, gave an address on Parry as a Three Choirs' man.

Following the excellent example set by Hereford many years before, the Gloucester Stewards decided to give a second secular concert in the Shire Hall on the Friday, and they were more than justified in their decision by the result, for the room was sold out some days in advance. The broadcasting of the evening concerts was another innovation, and gave immense pleasure to thousands of listeners in Gloucester alone who were unable to gain admission. Crowds of people assembled in various parts of the city where a loudspeaker was to be found, and listened most attentively to every item in the programmes. In this way the humblest citizen in Gloucester had the opportunity of 'standing room' at a Three Choirs Festival without fee or discomfort. The concluding voluntaries at this Festival at the close of the Three Choirs Services, as in 1922, were a feature, two having been specially written, by Alan Gray,[19] and Charlton Palmer[20] of Canterbury.

Before concluding my impressions of this Festival I should like again to speak of the warm-hearted and loyal support I received from the members of the chorus. They were ever ready to carry out my wishes, and too much praise cannot be given them for the part they played in the Festival. Not only were they generous in giving of their time and ability to the cause, but they were most generous in subscribing to a donation to the Charity Fund. It should be borne in mind that nearly all these enthusiastic singers *give* their services, and only a few receive a small sum towards their out-of-pocket expenses.

There was no lack of aspirants to join the chorus, many of whom were, of course, quite unqualified. One lady from a neighbouring town volunteered her services, and when she came for an interview I placed before her Bach's *Christmas Oratorio* and asked her to tell me the key of the first chorus. She thereupon solemnly turned over every page in the work, and then gave the wrong key! When she was

---

19   Dr Alan Gray (1855–1935) was Organist of Trinity College, Cambridge, from 1893 to 1930. See Shaw, *The Succession of Organists*, p.371.
20   Dr C. Charlton Palmer (1871–1944) was Organist of Canterbury Cathedral from 1908 to 1936. See Shaw, *op. cit.*, p.50.

Group photograph from *The Times* (1925), showing (l-r):
Sir Herbert Brewer, Sir Percy Hull (Organist of Hereford Cathedral),
The Very Rev'd Dr Henry Gee (Dean of Gloucester), Mr P. Barrett
Cooke (Festival Treasurer, and former Festival Secretary), Sir Edward
Elgar and Dr W. H. Reed.

Copyright holder untraced.

asked to read a short passage at sight from this work, she admitted that her reading was not as good as it was, as she had not practised for a month! She had brought a copy of the *Messiah* which she said she knew, and she thought I would like to hear her 'read' something from that work! She was a very accommodating person. When I asked her what she sang, she replied she could sing either soprano, alto, tenor or bass.

The sermon at the opening of the Festival was preached by the Bishop of Oxford (Dr Strong),[21] who, in reply to the few clergy who still object to the use of cathedrals for musical festivals, said, "While in the English Church painting and religion have long parted company, and religious poetry is only another way of saying bad poetry, music still keeps its ancient link with religion." I will also quote Dr Headlam,[22] Bishop of Gloucester, who does not sympathize with such criticism, and who feels that he can speak without prejudice, because there are few people, he thinks, to whom music appeals less than it does to himself. In a letter to the Press he writes:

> Music is for many one of the most potent of influences. Men's lives and conduct and spiritual attitude are influenced far more by their senses and emotions than by their reason, and music probably in its many forms of development is often a great power. It is important, therefore, that the Church should do all in its power to bring music, like the other great activities of life, under its influence, and to direct this powerful agent to a good purpose. A high standard of music in our churches will be encouraged by an exhibition of music of great beauty, beautifully rendered. Tradition is against those who object to such a festival taking place in a cathedral, and, I think, also common sense. In old days our cathedrals and churches were used for mystery plays and in many other ways which are not now customary. And is it not better that a great building like a cathedral, the only building of the size and construction fitted for the purpose, should be used in any way consistent with the purpose to which it is dedicated? We need not confine our religious services

---

21 Dr Thomas Banks Strong (1861–1944) later became Bishop of Oxford.
22 Dr Arthur Cayley Headlam CH (1862–1947), Regius Professor of Divinity at Oxford (1918–23), and Bishop of Gloucester from 1923 to 1945.

to what is usual and commonplace. I cannot feel the force
of the objection that is felt as to the charge for admission.
If any charge were made for attendance at the regular
services, or for any direct evangelical work, I should
strongly condemn it. But a musical festival of a religious
character is different. It makes a special appeal to special
people. There are ample opportunities for those who are
not wealthy to hear good music. The skilled musician is
as worthy of his hire as the skilled lawyer or doctor. All
that is received beyond the necessary expense is used for
an admirable purpose.

A month later he paid the following tribute to the Festival:

I think that all who were concerned with the Musical
Festival this year ought to receive high commendation
for the way in which the work was done. I have seldom
taken part in any such festival, or service, which was so
well organized, and good organization dealing with such
a large number of persons means infinite care. All the
testimony that I have received is to the effect that the
performance of the music was of the highest standard,
and in particular that the chorus was one of the best that
has been heard in the cathedral. That of course means
long, careful, and thoughtful preparation. Our musicians
set us a very good example of the way in which we should
do anything. We should take the greatest amount of
trouble to make it as good as possible. But what I am
most concerned with is the extreme reverence that was
shown by the whole attendance on all occasions when I
was present, and the many signs and evidences I have
had of the intense spiritual influence of the services. I see
no grounds at all for altering the judgment I have already
expressed, and I am sure that the critics of the Festival
hold a very narrow view of the functions of a cathedral.

Such high commendation coming from such a source will do
much to kill the narrow-minded view taken by those few who bring
forward their annual protest to these Music Meetings.

Many are the stories which go the round during the Festival
week. Here is one that appeared in a leading provincial paper under
the heading:

MAN WITH NO TICKET

Carrying out very explicit instructions that during the Three Choirs Festival no one was to pass through the cloisters of Gloucester Cathedral without a ticket, one of the doorkeepers stopped an individual who could not produce the necessary authority.

"Oh, it's all right," said the man, but the doorkeeper replied, "Is it? I've heard that tale before." And he proceeded to march him out of the cloisters. Only when the man turned round and said, "You are one of the best doorkeepers we have had on duty at these Festivals" did the doorkeeper recognize the Festival conductor. On the following afternoon the doorkeeper was sent for, and in place of the expected reprimand he received from Dr Brewer a signed photograph of himself as a mark of appreciation of loyalty to duty.

– 22 –

The final years

An Epilogue
by Ethel Mary Brewer

With some personal recollections
by W. H. Reed, M.V.O.

My husband's reminiscences came to an end in or about 1925, so it falls to me to complete the story with a brief record of the subsequent years and a few extracts from what was written about him by those who knew him intimately.

When considering the programme for the 1928 Festival, with his usual desire to attract worldwide interest, he wrote to Ravel in the hope of obtaining not only a novelty for the Festival but the presence of the great French composer to conduct his work. But Ravel, in quaint English, points out the reason of his inability to accept:

9 Rue Tourasse 9 St. Jean de Luz
September 2nd, 1927

Dear Sir

I have received your letter of August 29th in which you kindly ask me to write a new work for the THREE CHOIRS' FESTIVAL which is to be held in Gloucester in September, 1928. I thank you most sincerely for it but I am sorry to say that I think it impossible for me to write a new work, even a very short one, before that time, for I am very busy presently as I am leaving soon for America, and on my

return I'll have to end a very long and important work,
and will surely have no free time to write it till then.[1]
Really sorry,

Yours truly,

Maurice Ravel

It was at a Stewards' meeting on January 16th, 1928, that he submitted his sketch programme for the coming Festival. In doing so he mentioned that it had not been drawn up with hasty judgment, but was the outcome of months of thought; music, like other arts, did not stand still, and it was necessary to introduce all schools of thought and to satisfy all tastes, not forgetting to make the old masters the foundation of the programme. It was difficult to select from so many distinguished living composers, and it was impossible to include them all. They were fortunate in their novelties, for not only were they to have new works from Bantock, Holst, Ireland and others, but quasi-novelties from such men as Honegger and Kodály were included in the scheme. Elgar's name figured largely in the scheme; both architecturally and acoustically the Cathedral formed a more perfect setting for his music than any other place.

The programme submitted was as follows:

Sunday	Opening Service, *Andante con moto*, from the Symphony in C minor (Beethoven); Motet, *There is an old belief* (C. H. H. Parry).
Tuesday	New Orchestral Work (John Ireland); The Lord's Prayer (C. Lee Williams); New Motet, *Ye Choirs of New Jerusalem* (Basil Harwood); *Elijah* (Mendelssohn).
Tuesday Evening	New Orchestral Work (G. Holst); *Two Psalms* (G. Holst); *Gerontius* (Elgar).

---

1   Ravel was contemplating a four-month concert tour of America. In a letter to the French musicologist Henry Prunières dated only five days after his letter to Brewer, Ravel pointed out that "never having been there [i.e. America], I would be happy to see it". See Arbie Orenstein (ed.), *A Ravel Reader* (New York, 1990), p.280. Ravel's departure was apparently postponed, for he actually arrived in New York on 4 January 1928, returning to Le Havre on 27 April. The "very long and important work" requiring completion may have been *La Valse*, *Boléro*, or perhaps one of the two piano concertos.

Wednesday	Cantata, *O Light Everlasting* (Bach); *The Kingdom* (Elgar); New Work, *The Burden of Babylon* (Granville Bantock); Symphony in C (Schubert).
Wednesday Evening (Shire Hall)	'Cello Concerto (Elgar); Violin and Orchestra, *The Lark Ascending* (Vaughan Williams); New Orchestral Work (Honegger); Songs, etc.
Thursday	*Voces Clamantium* (Parry); Organ Concerto[2] (Handel); *Mass in D* (Ethel Smyth); *King David* (Honegger).
Thursday Evening	New Motet (Herbert Brewer); *Psalmus Hungaricus* (Zoltán Kodály); Rhapsody for Viola and Orchestra (W. H. Reed); *Requiem* (Verdi).
Friday	The *Messiah* (Handel).
Friday Evening (Shire Hall)	Songs (Schubert); Songs (Parry); Orchestral Works by Vaughan Williams,[3] Herbert Howells and Hathaway.[4]

Eventually Ireland, Holst and Honegger did not present new works, and at the Sunday Service Sullivan's *In Memoriam* Overture was played instead of Beethoven's *Andante con moto* in memory of Herbert Brewer. The Thursday evening programme was also made a special memorial performance by the inclusion of Lee Williams's unaccompanied anthem, *Thou wilt keep him in perfect peace*, sung in the distance by the cathedral choir, followed by the Motet, *God Within*, and at the end of the programme Verdi's *Requiem*. The Motet, *God Within*, had been written by request for the Festival of the Sons of the Clergy held in St Paul's Cathedral on May 9th, 1928, but the composer was destined never to hear it produced.[5]

---

2   Op.7, No.1 (in B flat), the only one of Handel's organ concertos with an independent pedal part.
3   *Charterhouse Suite.*
4   Hathaway's orchestral work *The Call of the Woods* received its first performance at the 1928 Gloucester Festival.
5   A comprehensive review by Harvey Grace of the 1928 Gloucester Festival was published in *Musical Times*, 69 (1928), pp.898–901.

The period following the Festival in 1925 was marked by various undertakings. In December of that year the 300th Free Recital in the Cathedral was made an occasion of special note, the performance being broadcast, and W. H. Reed was the solo violinist.

On New Year's Day[6] Herbert Brewer's name appeared in the Honours List, and on February 5th the King conferred the honour of Knighthood upon him.

In connection with the Bournemouth Festival in April, 1926, at which he conducted some of his own compositions, a clever and amusing caricature of him appeared in the *Daily News*, which is here reproduced.[7] He also took part in the opening celebrations of the new White Rock Pavilion at Hastings in April, 1927, and conducted his *England, my England*.

It was after the 1925 Festival that there were signs of failing health, and walking became more and more an effort. The Festival had undoubtedly been too great a strain, but his enthusiasm for work did not lessen, and in 1926, on the resignation of George Riseley from the conductorship of the Bristol Choral Society he was invited to undertake and accepted the duties of that office.

In December, 1927, at the Society's annual performance of the *Messiah* he had conceived the idea of inviting the audience to join in the *Hallelujah* chorus. The suggestion was received with some trepidation, but the venture justified itself, and the following account may be taken to voice the opinion of the audience as a whole:[8]

> "I can only say thank you. I think it is safe to say nothing has ever been heard like that in this country before," said Sir Herbert Brewer, greatly moved by what had just occurred, to an audience of over three thousand at Colston Hall, Bristol, on Saturday night.
>
> Sir Herbert had announced previously that he would ask the audience to rise and join in singing the Hallelujah Chorus.
>
> As a result of this the greater portion of the audience brought with them copies of the Messiah. He asked those

---

6   1926.

7   The caricature, which appeared in *The Daily News* on 8 April 1926, is facing p.224 in the 1931 edition of Brewer's *Memories*.

8   The source of this report has not been traced.

who knew the chorus and intended singing to do so with the reverence due to so great a work.

With the Society's chorus of 400, a full orchestra and the Colston Hall organ – one of the finest in this country[9] – the audience sang in perfect harmony. Sopranos, contraltos, tenors and basses, in all parts of the hall, sang their respective parts. Perfect time was kept, and so impressive was the rendering that many were in tears.

The climax came before the final Hallelujah. There was silence while Sir Herbert held his baton aloft for a second or two; then the four final chords crashed out with wonderful effect. Sir Herbert Brewer's daring experiment had been more than justified.

The works chosen for the final concert of the 1927–8 season were Verdi's *Requiem* and Dame Ethel Smyth's *Mass*, and only two days before his death, after a full day's work at Gloucester which included a choir practice, a rehearsal of the Orchestral Society, and the playing of the Cathedral Evensong, he motored to Bristol and conducted an unusually long rehearsal of the *Requiem* and *Mass*, afterwards motoring back to Gloucester. It was a tragic coincidence that the *Requiem* should have been included and ultimately retained in the programme, not to be directed by him but performed in his memory. And Verdi's *Requiem* of all others would have been his choice for his own requiem. He had been heard to say that if he was told to choose two works to hear before he died he would choose Verdi's *Requiem* and *The Dream of Gerontius*.

He had a great admiration for Verdi's music, and in a sense there must have been a similarity in their characters, for Giuseppina Strepponi[10] describes Verdi as an "iron nature who yet understood the most delicate as well as the most inspiring sentiment." And it was that iron nature combined with intense sensitiveness which were the secret of Herbert Brewer's power to lead and to draw the best out of those who came under his control.

---

9 The organ which Brewer would have known was a four-manual instrument by Willis, built for the re-opening of the hall in 1900 following its destruction by fire two years earlier. The organ was enlarged in 1905 by the firm of Norman and Beard.

10 Giuseppina Strepponi (1815–97), a renowned soprano from Lombardy, lived with Verdi from 1848 until 1859, in which year she became the composer's second wife.

He had a great love for the cathedral service, and his interest in it never tired. Only absence from home or an important engagement prevented his appearance in the organ-loft at the daily afternoon service. If the service went badly he would return home as depressed as he was elated if the choir had sung well. The psalms were his particular joy, and an enthusiastic parson from the north once described him as the king of psalm players. In his treatment of the choristers some may have considered him too severe, but the following appreciation by an old chorister in the *Musical Times* is an illustration of the regard felt by the choristers for their master:[11]

> To those who knew him intimately the unexpected news of Sir Herbert Brewer's death came as a grievous shock, bringing with it the feeling of a really personal loss. Those of us who had the privilege of serving under him at the noble Cathedral of Gloucester had the greatest possible affection and regard for him, both as a man and as a musician.
>
> [It was on December 15, 1896, that the then Mr Brewer was appointed organist and master of the choristers at Gloucester Cathedral in succession to Mr C. Lee-Williams, thus returning to the Cathedral in which, as a boy, he had sung from 1877 to 1880. In the matter of his appointment he had a most influential backing, amongst those who supported him being Stainer, Parratt, Parry, Bridge, Lloyd, and Lee Williams. In the light of after events it is interesting to recall some of the things that were said at this time regarding Brewer's qualifications for the position. Lloyd spoke of him as a capable choir-trainer, a successful composer, and a highly-accomplished organist, and, *inter alia*, he said, "It would, in my judgment, be difficult to find a man more thoroughly fitted for the duties of the important post which he seeks to fill."

---

11 This appreciation was abbreviated in the 1931 edition of Brewer's *Memories*. It is given here in full, as printed in *Musical Times*, 69 (1928), pp.315–16, with the restored passages enclosed in brackets. 'H. D.' identifies himself only as 'An Old Gloucester Cathedral Chorister'. He may have been Harry Dawes (see above, p.2, fn.4), whose father – Frank William Dawes (d.1938) – was a prominent Gloucestershire musician, and conducted the band of the Royal Gloucestershire Hussars.

Lee Williams spoke in a very similar vein, referring to his one-time deputy as a successful choir-trainer, and a first-rate Cathedral organist. How thoroughly Brewer merited these and other recommendations, and how completely his appointment was justified, are now matters of history.]

It was some eighteen months after Brewer's appointment to Gloucester that I first made his acquaintance. I well remember being taken to him by my father, who at that time was organist at one of the city's most important parish churches in the town, to undergo a test prior to joining the choir as a probationer, and I still retain a happy memory not only of his extreme kindness and interest on that occasion, but also of the thoroughness with which he tested my musical abilities. A good voice and a good ear were, of course, essentials for any budding chorister; but a practical knowledge of an instrument – it mattered not what – was a *sine qua non* of his ultimate approval.

[Memories of the seven happy years spent as a chorister at Gloucester come crowding to one's mind at this sorrowful moment; but space does not permit the mention of more than a few.]

Brewer had high ideals concerning the type of music worthy of performance in a place of worship, and he also had strong ideas regarding the performance of it. No unworthy music, no unworthy performance, was ever tolerated, and woe betide the person who tried to introduce either element into the worship music of the Cathedral. It was no unusual thing for the organ to stop suddenly during the service, and for a face to appear above the organ screen, gazing down – perhaps as much in sorrow as in anger – upon some delinquent who had done rather less than his best. And the end was certain. After the service one of the many articled pupils would inform us that our presence was required either in the practice-room, or (under more distressing circumstances) at the familiar study at Millers Green. And then the blow would fall. Brewer was a strict – almost severe – disciplinarian, and any departure from his rigid code always met with its deserts; but I never knew him act unjustly or unkindly to those serving under him. In spite of the rigidity of his discipline, which I am inclined now to think was commendable, he was at heart the most kind and genial of

men. His interest in one's youthful ambitions, whatever
may have been their nature, was almost paternal. Many
little efforts in composition, for example, were brought to
him from time to time by various choristers (myself for
one), and always he displayed the same generous interest
and the same ready desire to encourage and help. And so,
as the years passed, one's respect for the master gradually
merged into an abiding affection for the man.

Brewer was a man of few words, but every word had
significance. He knew exactly what he wanted; in some
magnetic way the idea was conveyed to the choir or
orchestra under his control; and he himself spared no
pains (or feelings, for that matter) in the effort to secure
the desired result. He worked as hard as any man I
have known, and he expected, and usually got, an equal
response from others. I recall a Shire Hall rehearsal for
the Three Choirs Festival (probably that of 1901) when the
heat was almost unbearable. But it never entered Brewer's
head to give up. First of all his coat was discarded, then the
waistcoat; the male members of the chorus followed suit,
and the rehearsal carried on to its appointed end.

Brewer's kindness to his choristers did not cease when
they left the choir; he always showed great interest in their
after career. Whenever one returned to Gloucester on rare
visits there was always the ready welcome and the kindly
interest in one's doings. I still treasure many letters from
him indicative of the warm interest and pleasure he felt in
the successes of his old boys. Few have greater cause than
they to remember with real and affectionate regard the
human and manly side of Sir Herbert's character.

[Only one organist of Gloucester Cathedral (William
Mutloe) held the position for a longer period than Brewer;
none of them, I venture to say, wielded a greater or more
far-reaching influence. He had many musical and other
interests outside the Cathedral; he served as City High
Sheriff with great distinction, 1922–23; and he remained
to the end one of Gloucester's most honoured citizens.
One other thing should be said: when Brewer took over
the conductorship of the Three Choirs Festival the meeting was by no means on a financially sound basis; he has
left it as one of the most prosperous and distinguished
of provincial festivals, which is a tribute not only to his
high musicianship, but also to his remarkable business

acumen. Some twenty-four thousand people attended the 1925 Festival, and no less than £3,737 was handed over to charity.

And now his ashes rest at the foot of the steps of the organ-loft which he adorned for so many years, and one's heart is too full to do more than echo the words of Canon Atlay,[12] in his sermon at Gloucester Cathedral on Sunday, March 4:[13] 'I beg you, with me, to commend to the Divine mercy the soul of Herbert Brewer, Knight Bachelor of the Realm: "Eternal rest grant unto him, O Lord, and let light perpetual shine on him"'.]

H. D.

His serene, quiet, self-possessed manner gave some people the impression that he was lacking in energy. On one occasion a post, which he had expressed a wish to hold, was given to another man, on the grounds that a man with energy was required. How little they knew him! Once having made up his mind to achieve an object no work would be too arduous for him to perform to obtain that goal. His characteristic determination and perseverance would be brought into play to surmount all difficulties.

The astonishing succession of financial and attendance records of the Gloucester Festivals was in a great measure due to his untiring energy. For each of the post-war Festivals he wrote some hundreds of letters with his own hand inviting people to become Stewards, and so keen was he to attract newcomers, that whenever he made new acquaintances a note was made of their names and addresses, and in due course they received letters inviting them to become Stewards of the Festival.

No details were too small to command his attention, and his thought and consideration for the comfort and well-being of all connected with the Festivals played no small part in the smooth-working and consequent enjoyment of the Festivals by all concerned.

To these characteristics, W. H. Reed bears testimony in the following recollections of his old friend.

---

12 Canon Marcus Ethelbert Atlay (1881–1934) was a Residentiary Canon at Gloucester Cathedral from 1923 to 1934. He was the son-in-law of Lord Merrivale.

13 The Sunday following Brewer's death.

A good many years have passed since Sir Alexander Mackenzie sent for me to know if I would consider taking up some work in Gloucester.

I was then a student at the R.A.M. and was very excited at the prospect. I found my services were required to help Mr Brewer (as he then was) to train a County Orchestral Society. He wanted a young man with plenty of energy to go round the county to form sub-centres, and conduct rehearsals in Stroud, Berkeley, Cheltenham, Newnham-on-Severn, Tewkesbury, etc., to lead at a combined practice once a month under his conductorship at Gloucester, and to lead at the Concerts.

This seemed at the time a most exciting and interesting appointment. The only thing was, I had never met Brewer, nor had he ever seen or even heard of me.

The day arrived for me to go to Gloucester to lead at a grand opening rehearsal. Brewer conducted. He made me feel at once that I should be happy in the new environment.

After the rehearsal we went back to his house in Palace Yard, as it was called in those days, where we had tea, and he and I played a Grieg Sonata for Violin and Piano.[14]

Little did I think how much at home I was destined to be in that house. From the first day a firm and staunch friendship commenced between us which lasted without any suspicion of a cloud until the day of his death.

I had not been working with him long before he bade me walk into the house at all times, without troubling to ring the bell, or letting anyone know I was coming. "You are always welcome here, and there is always a bed for you."

Well, there *was*, and if there was ever a more hospitable household than that in this world I have yet to find it.

If I were asked what characteristic of Brewer remains most firmly in my mind I should say his inflexible loyalty. He never forgot if any one did him some service or helped him in any way, nor did he rest until he had managed to do something in return. The next thing was his pertinacity. If he had an idea and thought it was a good one, he would pursue it through thick and thin until he was successful,

---

14	Grieg's three Violin Sonatas – Op.8, Op.13 and Op.45 – were composed between 1865 and 1887.

whether it was to build a new organ in the Shire Hall,[15] or to do something for the advancement of some friend or one of his pupils.

In the summer evenings, after our work was done, we used to walk out in the meadows, and on these walks he used to open his heart to me. He was always planning something to help someone. No one apart from his own family, and, I believe, myself, will ever know how warm-hearted he was, as all his generous acts were done quietly and unobtrusively.

Another, and perhaps his most lovable, quality was his perfect simplicity. He loved all things in nature – he loved going round by the osier beds, noting how the Severn came round the bend, and would get quite excited when it overflowed and flooded the meadows, and sent me postcards to say how deep it was, and still rising. "Only a few yards now from Palace Yard," and then it froze, and the whole of Gloucester went out there to skate. How he loved his Gloucester people and everything in the city, but most of all the Cathedral! When out walking, we always had to turn every now and again to see how it looked from this or that point of view, perhaps in the rays of the setting sun, or in the moonlight. Then nearly always, if it were not actually raining, we had to go into Palace Yard to stand in silence and look up at the Tower before we went to our beds.

He was loyal to his friends, he loved his Cathedral, he was simple-minded and generous, and when I lost him I lost the best friend any man could have.

W. H. R.

A marked trait in his character – unusual in a musician – was his extraordinary business instinct. He would not be happy if any Society with which he was connected was in financial straits, and he would not rest until that Society had been put on its feet again and had a small nest egg in the bank. However much he might want to perform a big work requiring many artists and a full orchestra, he would not suggest its performance unless he could see his way to make both ends meet.

---

15 See p.104, fn.11.

This business instinct showed itself particularly in his personal investments. To give an instance, he once commissioned his lawyer to go to a very large sum for the purchase of a small property, in spite of the fact that the necessary money had to be borrowed. Moreover, it was quoted as the highest price hitherto paid for a property of its size in Gloucester. But his judgment had not been at fault, for at his death it was valued at nearly twice the original cost.

He was a born organizer, and this gift was brought into play when arranging programmes of concerts and festivals. He always strove to make them as varied as possible, to please all tastes and to avoid monotony. Perhaps it was this aptitude for gauging the public taste that accounted for the tribute of praise accorded him by the critic of *The Observer* after a performance of some of his own works at the B.B.C. studio in Birmingham in November, 1927. He says:

> Occasionally the B.B.C. ladle out "Hours with" contemporary or classical composers – an ordeal out of which even masters like Mozart and Tchaikovsky do not come unscathed. Perhaps choice of items may have something to do with it, for Sir Herbert Brewer's hour last Thursday (which he arranged and conducted himself) was above expectation.
>
> The music is thoroughly English, pleasant to listen to, bright and vigorous, saying what it has to say well, and not bothering about its immortal soul, which is the best proof that it has got one. It was all well conducted, played and sung.

A very true description of him as a public character appeared in the *Musical Times* for April, 1928. It ran as follows:

> There will always be differing views as to this country's ability to produce a wealth of outstanding composers or interpretative artists; national characteristics are perhaps against us here. But there is one type of musician in which we seem almost to specialize: the all-rounder who is also a practical man of affairs. His evolution is no doubt due to the centralization of the musical life of a town or district round the parish church or cathedral – a principle which seems to obtain more generally in this country than in any other, probably because the one department of music

in which England has had an unbroken tradition for centuries is that of the Church. Those out of sympathy with the product of this system will call him a Jack-of-all-trades (with the usual implication of lack of thoroughness); generally, however, he deserves the title of Admirable Crichton.

Sir Herbert Brewer was a fine example of this invaluable type. An admirable organist and choirmaster, he was no less successful as a conductor and organizer. His work in connection with, *e.g.*, the Gloucester Orchestral Society and the Bristol Choral Society would alone have been sufficient to show his qualities in this way. But they were demonstrated even more strikingly in connection with the Three Choirs Festival. Here he showed a spirit of enterprise that was acknowledged even by those who take the conventional and short-sighted view of the Cathedral organ-loft as a kind of last ditch of the reactionist and pedant. A list of new and unfamiliar works that have been included in the Gloucester Festivals on Brewer's initiative would put to shame the record of many a provincial Festival that prides itself on its enterprise. (In this connection we note with interest the comparison which Dr Herbert Thompson[16] draws in the *Yorkshire Post* between the courage and vision of Brewer at Gloucester and the timid policy of the Leeds Festival executive.)

That the daring shown in the drafting of the Festival programmes was justified by results was due largely to the influence of Sir Herbert's personality and to his ability as an organizer. Without these his excursions into the unfamiliar might have proved disastrous, especially as his boldest steps were taken during the post-war period when, if ever, conductors would appear to be justified in playing for safety. Yet the Three Choirs Festival is to-day one of the most flourishing and securely established musical events in the country, and one which moreover in an unusual degree commands the suffrages of musicians who like to label themselves as progressive. For this happy state of affairs Sir Herbert's colleagues at Worcester and Hereford are also to be thanked, but we think they will readily give

16 Dr Herbert Thompson (1856–1945) was music and art critic of the *Yorkshire Post* from 1886 to 1936.

the major part of the credit to him, both on the score of wide outlook and of experience. (With one exception, he had conducted more Three Choirs Festivals than any other man during their two centuries of existence.)

As a composer Sir Herbert almost inevitably produced choral works for use at the Festivals. His real bent, however, lay rather towards a lighter style. In his songs and instrumental pieces, especially those produced during the past few years, he discovered a vein of tunefulness that we associate especially with Sullivan and German. This side of his activity is of interest, as exemplifying the ease with which he avoided the limited outlook which is always a danger to the occupant of the organ-loft. In a sense it is a corollary of the enterprise that led to his choice for Festival programmes of such works as Kodály's *Psalmus Hungaricus*, new orchestral compositions by Ireland, Holst, Honegger, and Vaughan Williams's *The Lark Ascending*, all of which are included in the scheme for the next Gloucester meeting.[17]

The many warm personal tributes that have been uttered during the past few weeks are a striking testimony to his worth as a man. This is not the place, however, to discuss the personal side of Brewer. Our concern is rather with the public character. Proverbially no man is indispensable, but some are difficult to replace. Such a man was Alfred Herbert Brewer. A fine musician, and a stimulating and directing power in the artistic life of a wide area, his death leaves a gap hard to fill.[18]

It was a strange coincidence that on the first Thursday in March, 1897, Herbert Brewer began his duties as organist in Gloucester Cathedral by playing the organ at a Free Recital, and it was on the first Thursday in March, 1928, thirty-one years later, whilst the Concert of the Gloucestershire Orchestral Society was in progress,

---

17 Ireland, Holst and Honegger all failed to produce a new work for the 1928 Festival. Holst's *Two Psalms*, which had been performed at the 1922 Gloucester Festival, were repeated in 1928. Honegger was represented exclusively by *King David*, which had been in Brewer's original plan anyway.

18 This notice was printed in the original edition of Brewer's *Memories of Choirs and Cloisters* in a slightly truncated form. It is given here in full, as printed in *Musical Times*, 69 (1928), p.315.

Sir Edward Elgar (centre) arriving to attend the interment of Sir Herbert Brewer's ashes at Gloucester Cathedral on Tuesday 6 March 1928 (Sir Herbert had been cremated the previous day at Perry Barr Crematorium, Birmingham). The party, led by Charles Lee Williams, is seen walking across College Green. On Elgar's left is Theodore Hannam-Clark, a member of the Executive Committee of the Three Choirs Festival. In the background is the Chapter House, and behind it the schoolhouse on the corner of College Court.

Photograph originally published in the *Cheltenham Chronicle and Gloucestershire Graphic*, Saturday 10 March 1928.
Reproduced by permission of Gloucestershire Archives.

that he lay dying. Almost his last words were, "I feel as if I were conducting the symphony." Mozart's Symphony in E flat[19] was then actually in progress. Before its conclusion he had gone forward to carry on his work in wider spheres untrammelled by an earthly body.

Truly a merciful passing. A recovery from that first attack of angina pectoris would have meant a life deprived of all work, and to a man devoted to his work, whose work, as he was wont to say, was his hobby, such a life would have been worse than death.

His ashes were laid to rest beneath a stone at the foot of the steps to the organ-loft he loved so well, and his memory is perpetuated in a window in the Musicians' Chantry in the Lady Chapel of the Cathedral,[20] and by a Scholarship for Gloucester Choristers adopting music as a profession.

---

19 Symphony No.39 (K.543).
20 Other local musicians who are commemorated in windows in the South Chantry of the Lady Chapel at Gloucester include S. S. Wesley, Parry, Herbert Sumsion and Herbert Howells.

Index of compositions

Index